MW01709014

A Guide to the

Prevention *and* Treatment *of* Back Pain

A Guide to the

Prevention *and* Treatment *of* Back Pain

DR JOSHUA RAJ

ARMOUR

Published by ARMOUR Publishing Pte Ltd
Kent Ridge Post Office
P. O. Box 1193, Singapore 911107
Email: mail@armourpublishing.com
Website: www.armourpublishing.com

15 14 13 12 11
5 4 3 2 1

Disclaimer:
This book serves as a general guide for readers to have a better understanding of back pain and its treatment. However, the materials in this book are not intended to replace professional medical care or attention provided by a qualified practitioner. It cannot and should not be used as a basis for diagnosis or choice of treatment for an individual. The mention of any product, service or treatment should not be considered as endorsement by the authors or publisher. Readers are advised to consult their respective doctors and healthcare professionals regarding specific management strategies for their own medical conditions. The publisher, the author(s) or anyone involved in the production of this book is not responsible for any adverse consequence caused by any person reading or following the materials in this book.

Printed in Singapore

ISBN 13: 978-981-4305-32-7
ISBN 10: 981-4305-32-4

National Library Board, Singapore Cataloguing-in-Publication Data

Raj, Joshua.
A guide to the prevention and treatment of back pain / Joshua Raj. –
Singapore : Armour Pub., c2011.
p. cm.
Includes index.
ISBN : 978-981-4305-32-7 (pbk.)

1. Backache – Treatment. 2. Backache – Prevention. I. Title.

RD771.B217
617.564 -- dc22 OCN713004566

Contents

1 Introduction

This book is a response to a need my patients have always expressed — an explanation for why they have back pain and what they should do about it. Their enquiries and bemused expressions are in my mind as I pen this book. Many of their questions were surprisingly similar, indicating that there is a body of information in the community, some of which is correct, but others erroneous yet believed and acted upon. There is also confusion over the proliferation of therapies and healing practitioners. It has become the vogue to disparage allopathic medicines and surgery, while unsuspectingly embracing unproven claims and "new" therapies.

Over the years, I have seen thousands of patients with back pain. Some recover after one visit while others have been on follow-up for some time. Have you ever wondered why different doctors (and alternate practitioners) give different advice for the same backache? Even contradictory and opposite advice!

Firstly, there is no single cause for low back pain. There are hundreds of possible causes. Secondly, a specific treatment may not have the same effect in every patient. Each patient is an individual and does not react the same way to a therapy. Thirdly, evidence-based medical studies (studies of large numbers of patients) are debunking myths about which treatments work and which do not. Even medical, rehabilitation and surgical advice is changing based on new evidence. With time, all treatment practices that are anecdotal (based on personal experience or hearsay) will be scrutinised for their effectiveness.

Back pain? Please be patient with your doctor. If you are not patient, you could end up going to several doctors, acupuncturists, physiotherapists, chiropractors, osteopaths, traditional medicine and massage. You would have spent a lot of time and money, and still have back pain.

This book is meant to raise your awareness of some of the recent common practices in the treatment of low back pain so that you make informed treatment decisions. But remember, this book is only meant to equip you with information. When in doubt, see a doctor. **Do not self diagnose and treat yourself without a proper assessment.**

Dr JR Raj
MD, FRCSEd, AMM, FICS

2

Quick Guide Chart

Quick Guide to Treatment Options for Low Back Pain

The treatment options of non-specific back pain without obvious bone/cartilage problems are:

Sudden, Severe Back Pain

Very helpful	Painkillers (tablets, suppositories or injection) Bed rest for a short time Cold pack
Helpful	Non-Steroidal Anti-Inflammatory medicine (NSAID) Muscle relaxant tablets Liniment or ointments
Not helpful	Physiotherapy Prolonged bed rest

Recent Non-specific, Moderate Low Back Pain

Very helpful	Non-Steroidal Anti-Inflammatory medicine (NSAID) Muscle relaxant tablets

	Back muscle strengthening exercises Spinal stretching exercises Trigger point injection and/or prolotherapy
Helpful	Physiotherapy-deep heat (ultrasound, short wave or microwave) Trigger point manipulation/massage therapy Acupressure/acupuncture (with current)

Chronic Non-specific, Moderate Low Back Pain

Very helpful	Back muscle strengthening exercises Spinal stretching exercises Trigger point injection and/or prolotherapy
Helpful	Non-Steroidal Anti-Inflammatory medicine Gabapentins (e.g. Neurontin tablets) Physiotherapy-deep heat (ultrasound, short wave or microwave) Trigger point manipulation/massage therapy Vitamin B6 and B12 supplements Epidural injection (if there is also leg pain)
May help	Anti-stress medications Counselling and biofeedback pain control Acupressure/acupuncture Transutaneous Electrical Nerve Stimulation (TENS)

Quick Guide to the Prevention of Low Back Pain

Normal Person (No Previous Low Back Pain)

Very helpful	Daily back stretches Correct posture (especially sitting) Proper footwear General fitness regime (e.g. aerobic exercises)
Helpful	Proper lifting and carrying of loads Moderately firm mattress and proper sleeping positions Daily back muscle strengthening exercises Maintain optimal body weight Regular general medical check up Reduce stress (work stress, relationship problems)
Not very helpful	Vitamins and various advertised supplements Expensive mattresses and electric beds

Chronic Back Pain (To Reduce Recurrence of Back Pain)

Very helpful	Daily back stretches (as recommended by doctor) Daily back muscle strengthening exercises Correct posture (especially sitting and standing) Proper footwear Proper lifting technique and carrying of loads Moderately firm mattress and comfortable sleeping positions Reduce weight if necessary
Helpful	Treat any general medical conditions (e.g. diabetes, gout) Minimise stress (work stress, relationship problems)

	Vitamins and medically prescribed supplements Anti-stress medication TENS machine (home models)
Sometimes helpful	Anti-inflammatory and muscle relaxant medications Heating pads and infra-red lamps
Not very helpful	Expensive mattresses, electric beds and chairs Unproven advertised supplements Over-the-Counter Back Supports

Section I

The Diagnosis of Low Backache

3

The Problem of Low Back Pain

What is the Extent of the Backache Problem in Modern Society?

Low back pain is one of the commonest problems seen by orthopaedic surgeons today. It is estimated that 85% of people will experience low backache lasting more than two weeks once in their life.

Medical leave for back pain accounts for almost half of the compensation (e.g. SOCSO) and insurance forms in my practice. In the USA, 25% of all worker compensation claims are due to backache. Medical leave due to backache is second only to broken bones. Many patients were taken off from work for six weeks, and still complain of pain!

Patients have a lot of misinformation and misconceptions about back pain. There are so many books, articles and stories that it is easy to get confused, even scared. This can result from the extremes of believing in exaggerated claims of success to unfounded fears of impending paralysis.

Before going into the details of the causes and treatment of backache, I will outline some of the more common misconceptions that come up when patients come to see me.

What are the Misconceptions about Low Back Pain?

Misconception 1: Once you get low back pain, you will have a permanent backache.

Many doctors did think that "once a back pain, always a back pain". We now know that this is not true for the majority of cases. Up to 90 percent of patients will recover whether they are treated or not. It is a very small number who actually end up in a doctor's office again. There is also no compelling evidence that a sudden back pain that goes away after two or three days will become chronic and permanent.

I encourage patients to resume normal activity as early as they can, with appropriate temporary medications and therapy, and within the limits of their discomfort. The majority of patients never suffer from back pain again. I advise them to forget that they even had back pain.

Misconception 2: Every backache patient needs an X-ray, CT or MRI scan.

Only some patients who have certain specific findings on examination require X-rays. Research has shown that up to thirty percent of MRI scans of people who have no backache will have an abnormal result. This means that an abnormal MRI or CT scan can be misleading and lead to unnecessary treatment, even surgery.

In cases where there is an obvious cause for the pain, like a fall or an accident, an X-ray is all that is needed. An MRI scan is done only if there are specific physical signs or factors like nerve compression signs that are not recovering after simple treatments, weakness of the legs (paralysis) associated with difficulty in passing urine or passing motion.

Misconception 3: Backache is caused by a "dislocation" of the bone of the spine.

There has always been confusion between the definition of the word "dislocation" and "subluxation". "Dislocation" simply means completely out of place, while "subluxation" means partly out of place. Only a severe accident or fall from a height can "dislocate" the spine bones. Many patients think that if they bend over, hear a "pop" sound and feel a backache, then something has "dislocated". This is reinforced by the meaning given to subluxation/dislocation by alternate medical practitioners.

The vertebrae cannot be dislocated or subluxed so easily, for example, by just bending over. The "pop" sound in the joint of the spine is similar to the sound which occurs when you crack your finger joints. There is a noise but the finger does not "dislocate". The wrong treatment will be to "push" or "manipulate" the spine back into place. The proper treatment is to allow time to heal, taking a short course of painkillers if necessary.

Misconception 4: If the back pain persists for a long time (chronic), surgery is needed.

"Do I need an operation?" is one of the first questions patients ask me. Surgery is done for specific reasons and very few patients need an operation. An operation is considered only after all other treatments have been tried. Patients must learn to be patient and not shop around for doctors after the first consultation.

I start with simple treatments and, if the patient is not better, follow up with other special treatments like physiotherapy and trigger point therapy. The patient may need a regular check up after a week or two. Failure to recover may require specialised non-operative treatments like trigger point injections and prolotherapy. Unfortunately, some patients forego their follow up and seek other treatment options if they are not better. Some feel it is costly to return for a check-up. But going from doctor to doctor will cost more in the long run, and the back pain may still persist.

Misconception 5: Backache must be caused by some injury to the bones and cartilage of the back.

"Do I need an X-ray?" is another common question. In reality, most back pain problems are actually due to muscle problems and weak ligaments. Structural problems with the bones and cartilage are not as common as is supposed. One study found that X-rays were useful in less than 5% of patients if done at the first consultation for non-specific pain.

This misconception about the bones is why many backache sufferers end up spending months on futile treatments. Even when an MRI scan reveals some bone/cartilage abnormality, it does not mean that this is the cause of the backache. We need to look at the patient more holistically and exclude some of the following problems:

- Poor general health or medical conditions like gout or diabetes which can contribute to non-specific back pain of muscle or tissue origin.

- Stress can aggravate or cause the back pain. Just as patients are known to get a headache or stomach ache when they are stressed, anxiety, stress and depression can be a cause of backache. This may be called fibromyalgia, myofascial pain or tension myositis syndrome by different practitioners. The mechanism of back pain may be due to an inflammation in the muscles caused by tension and stress.

Misconception 6: If there is backache, the bones must be "weak".
Some young women ask me whether they need to take calcium for weak bones, even though this is more a problem with older patients. "Weak bones" or osteoporosis generally affects older people (especially women) over the age of 50. So for younger patients, the causes are more likely to be one of the other structures (muscles and ligaments) in the spine. X-rays and bone density scans can reveal if osteoporosis is one of the causes of the pain.

Misconception 7: A lumbar back support is necessary for chronic back pain.
In fact, patients often walk into the clinic carrying a lumbar support belt, and tell me it is uncomfortable or not very useful. Many patients buy these back supports from the pharmacy on the notion that it is helpful to "support" the back. This is a misconception.

Lumbar back supports should be avoided, except for fracture treatment or after surgery. Patients using them should try to remove them as soon as possible. Recent studies prove that a back support is of little help for chronic backache sufferers. Prolonged use of a back support actually weakens the back muscles, and may prolong the backache.

Custom-made back braces can help for certain conditions. If necessary, it should be prescribed by a specialist and custom made for each patient.

Misconception 8: Alternative techniques, new machines and appliances, and/or recently discovered "wonder" supplements, diets or holistic medicine are better than regular medicines and/or physiotherapy treatment.

I suggest that you have a healthy scepticism towards those who claim that they have "new" cures for back pain. This includes both allopathic and alternate medicine practitioners. Be careful of books and advertisements claiming excellent and unrealistic results. What is often described as holistic or alternate treatment is usually a mixture of all kinds of fads and pseudoscience. Many companies advertise new "treatments" for all kinds of equipment and therapies, with little evidence for their efficacy. You must ask whether a treatment has been proven to be useful or whether it is just a claim made by a company to sell a product. Some practitioners make selective use of medical research to make a remedy appear "scientific". I would advise you to look at the totality (pros and cons) of medical research when evaluating a treatment modality.

Holistic treatment is a good concept. It means that doctors must look at more than just the anatomic structures of the spine (e.g. bones, joints and muscles), but also look at emotional issues, general health and nutrition. But just because someone claims a treatment is "holistic" does not mean it is useful. Many treatments like special beds, magnets, rays, lamps, pills containing all kinds of exotic things are advertised, but are often ineffective or bring only temporary relief.

In conclusion, remember that most acute back pains will recover whatever the treatment given. Always start with the simplest treatment.

Do not get worried, anxious or depressed when a backache occurs for the first time. Keeping a positive attitude, looking after your general health, and following a nutritious diet, simple muscle strengthening and spine flexibility instructions will lead to a good recovery. A summary of the usual treatment options is given in the Quick Guide Chart.

4

The Causes of Low Back Pain

What is Meant by Low Back Pain (Backache)?

Low back pain is a pain or ache that occurs mainly in the lower part of the spinal column (Photo 4.1). It can be ***acute*** (recent onset) or ***chronic*** (long time). The treatment of sudden back pain is very different from chronic back pain.

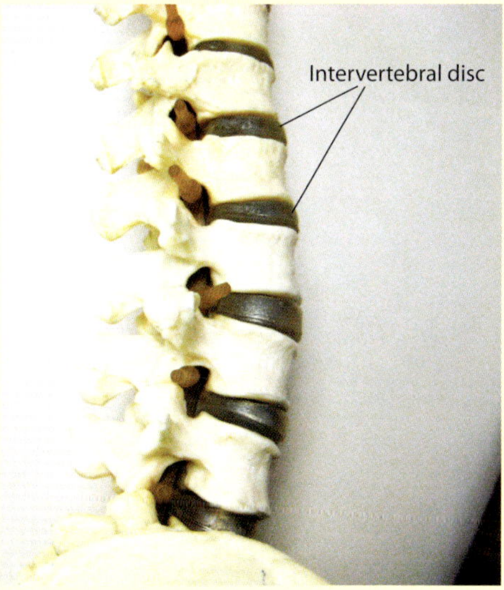

Photo 4.1: Lumbar Spine Model

The model shows the relationship of each vertebra and the intervertebral disc. The nerves come out behind the disc, through an opening called the intervertebral foramen.

It shows how close the nerve is to the intervertebral disc and why a small protrusion of the disc causes nerve compression.

Any disturbance to the normal alignment of the spine or the "spring" action to the discs may result in chronic back pain.

There are characteristics of the pain that help a doctor identify the cause. The history is important. When you see the doctor, try to remember what happened from the first time you experienced the pain.

What are the Common Causes of Back Pain?

Low back pain has many causes, from the common to the very rare. The common causes of backache discussed below cover more than ninety percent of back pain seen in my clinic.

Doctors (or traditional medicine) may give you different causes of the pain. This is because the cause can be difficult to diagnose even for professionals. Sometimes, it takes two or three visits before an effective treatment is found.

The common causes of backache can arise from three areas:

- **Anatomical Structure Problems** — the commonest area where pain originates is the physical body tissues and bones of the spine. Muscle pain is probably the major cause of non-specific back pain. There is a lot of overlap between structural problems with general health and stress problems.

- **General Health Problems** — pain may be part of another medical condition or made worse by poor health that causes inflammation and/or weakness of the tissues of the spine.

- **Stress-related Problems** — the daily anxiety and stresses of life can contribute to and even cause back pain, especially by increasing muscle tension.

Anatomical Body Structure Problems

The following physical structures in the body can cause backache when they are injured or damaged.

The Cartilage (Intervertebral Discs)

The cartilage between the vertebral bones of the spine (called

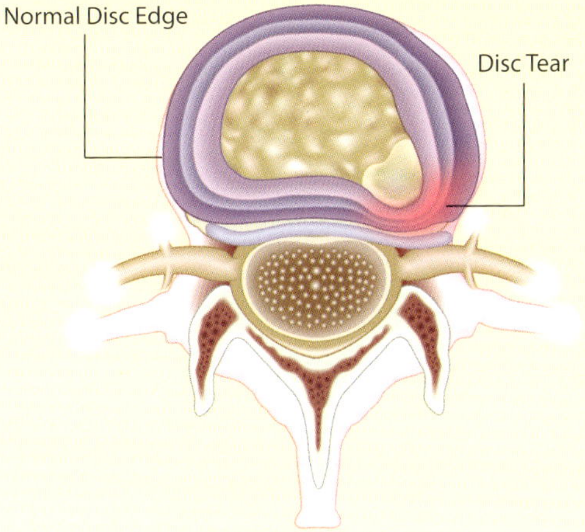

Diagram 4.2: Disc Tear
The intervertebral disc consists of an inner soft fleshy tissue (nucleus pulposus) surrounded by a firm fibrous ring (annulus fibrosus). When there is an injury, a small tear develops in the outer ring, allowing some of the inner fleshy material to protrude out. If the tear is complete, then inner material is pushed out and presses on the nerve.

intervertebral discs) acts as shock absorbers. The disc has a soft centre and a firm covering. The discs cushion the impact of daily activities on the bones of the spine.

Injury to the discs can cause pain in the following ways:

- **Disc Tear** — a tear in the disc covering (Diagram 4.2), caused by a sudden injury, can result in severe backache. With simple rest and painkillers, these tears heal very well.

- **Disc Prolapse** — ("slipped disc") — where some of the soft inner cartilage is squeezed out through a tear in the covering of the disc (Diagrams 4.3 and 4.4). This extruded disc material causes pain in the back, and even pain on one side of the leg. If only small amounts are extruded, these disc injuries can recover with simple treatment such as taking painkillers and/or muscle relaxants, rest and back exercises. If a lot of disc material is squeezed out, it may press on a nerve. Some patients may even have a piece of disc tissue completely detached and lying free in the spinal canal. These situations may need surgery if there is no improvement after simple treatments.

Diagram 4.3: Intervertebral Disc Prolapse

A. Mild Disc Prolapse

B. Severe Disc Prolapse

C. Loose Disc Fragment in Spinal Canal

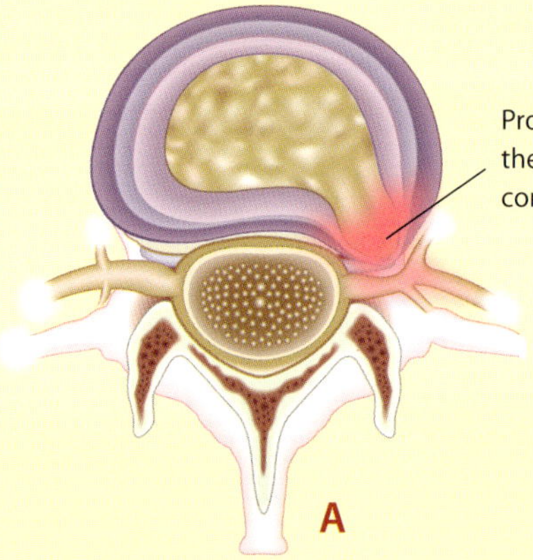

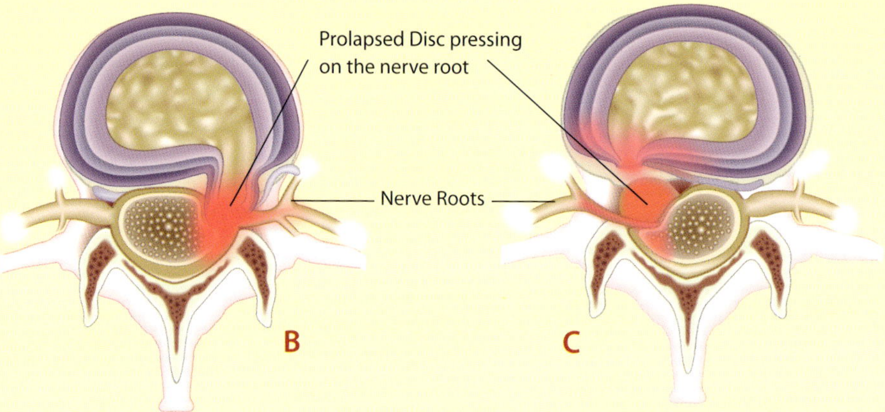

Disc prolapse can be of varying severity. Type A will cause mainly back pain. Type B and C will cause back and leg pain on the same side. Type B may sometimes recover with rest and usual non-operative treatment. Type C is unlikely to recover with medication alone, since the fragment is loose in the spinal canal.

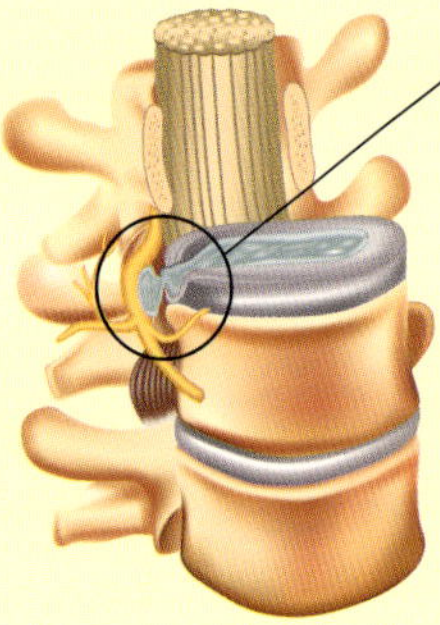

Diagram 4.4: Disc Prolapse

This model shows the side view of a disc prolapse and how the protrusion of the tissue presses on the nerve at the opening through which the nerves leave the spinal canal. Since the opening (foramen) is a fixed size, the nerve has to accommodate the smaller space.

- **Disc Degeneration** — as patients age, the disc cartilage tends to wear out and dry up ("wear and tear" changes). Pain can be caused by direct bone contact and/or grinding between the bones (Diagram 4.5). Disc degeneration can be particularly painful in the active years of life (30 to 50 years), and may become chronic but less painful as the patient gets older. The X-ray appearance and clinical symptoms often do not correlate — there can be severe X-ray degeneration with minimal backache and vice versa. We sometimes have to exclude other causes of pain before blaming the symptoms on degeneration.

The Bones (Lumbar Vertebra)

The spine is made up of "vertebra" bones that are stacked on one another. In patients with low backache, it is the lower five lumbar vertebra that may cause the pain (Photo 4.6 and Diagram 4.7).

- **Fractures:** Bones that are broken (e.g. due to an accident or a fall) or crushed (e.g. osteoporosis) can cause pain (Diagram 4.8 and Photo 4.9).

- **Dislocation:** Dislocation of the bones refers to bones slipping out of place. Because of the strong ligaments and cartilage discs of the spine, it requires a great injury force (like a high speed car accident or a fall from a high tree) to cause dislocation (Photo 4.10).

- **Subluxation**: Subluxation refers to a slight movement of one bone on another (Diagram 4.11). The common causes are usually congenital (born with some bone weakness) like spondylolysis or spondylolisthesis. It is a cause of back pain in younger patients, including teenagers. Those involved in sports have a higher incidence of back pain from this cause. Without surgery, it is not possible to push the bone back into place due to the abnormality in the bone or ligaments. However, many people with a mild spondylolisthesis have no pain at all.

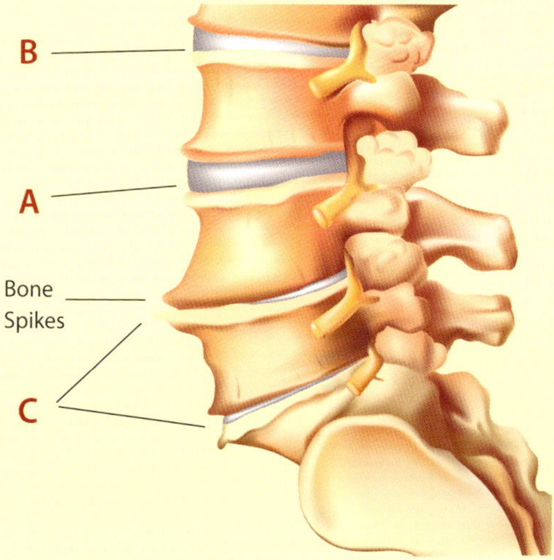

Diagram 4.5: Degeneration of Lumbar Spine

A. Mild Degeneration
B. Moderate Degeneration
C. Severe Degeneration

Note: Bone Spikes form due to the degeneration of the discs.

Degeneration of the intervertebral discs and the facet joints are part of the wear and tear process that comes with age. Note that the loss of intervertebral space is like the loss of the "spring". The bones can grind on each other, causing pain. The opening through which the nerves leave the spine are also narrowed. Patients can thus experience leg pain in addition to back pain.

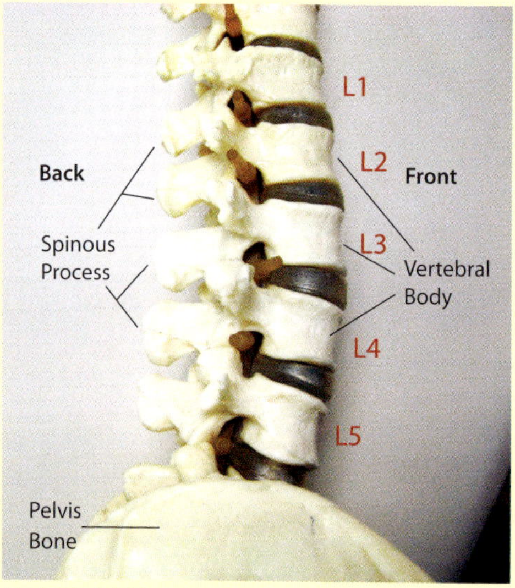

Photo 4.6: The Lumbar Vertebra

This model of the lumbar spine shows the area that is the source of any structural causes of low back pain. Normally, there are five lumbar vertebra, numbered as shown. The structures commonly involved are marked.

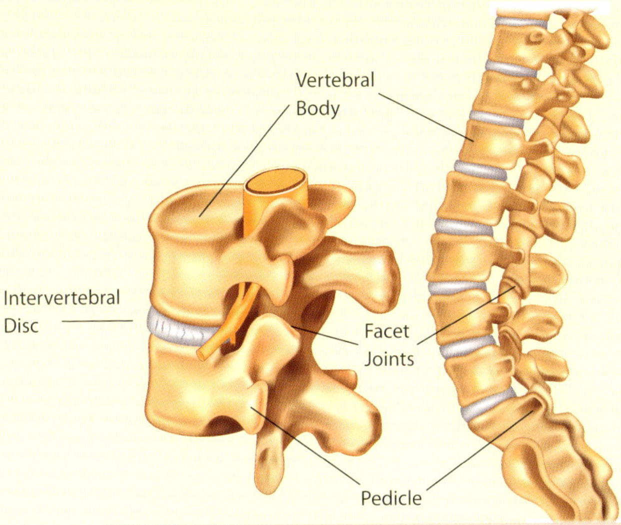

Diagram 4.7: The Lumbar Spine

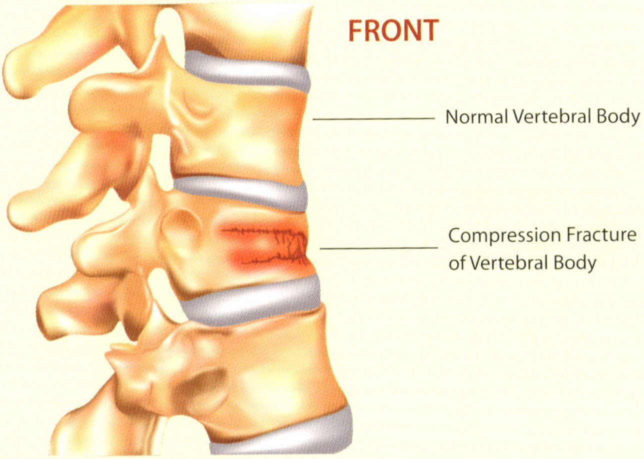

Diagram 4.8: Compression Fracture Lumbar Vertebra

The common fracture affecting the lumbar spine is a compression fracture, as shown in this model. The bones may go out of place, but that requires severe injuries from a fall or road accident. That is called a fracture dislocation.

Note that a fracture of this nature causes a change in the alignment of the spine. The body weight will run through the front of the disc rather than through the centre.

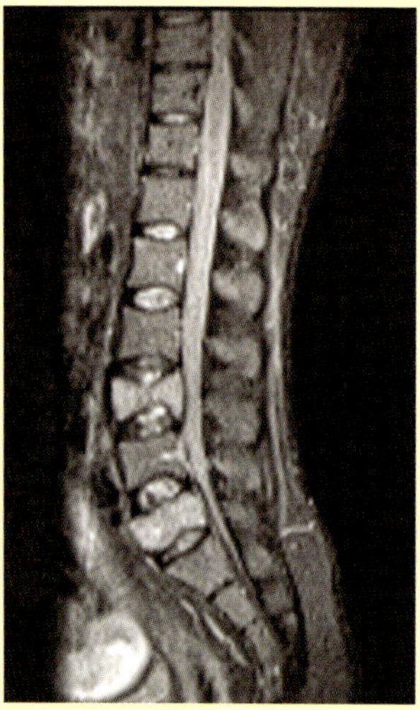

Photo 4.9: Compression Tear of Vertebra
An MRI of a compression fracture of vertebra. Healing is usually not complicated but the alignment of the spine is changed. The body weight may be shifted to the front, putting pressure on the adjacent intervertebral discs. There is also increased stress on the muscles and ligaments of the back, which can be a cause of chronic back pain.

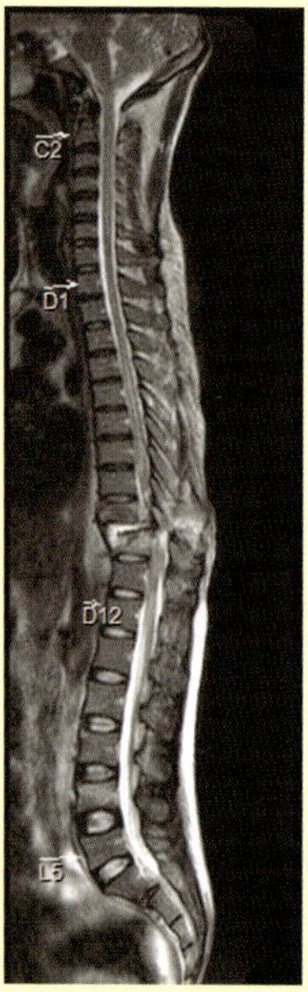

Photo 4.10: Fracture with Dislocation of Spine
An MRI scan showing a fracture combined with forward movement of the spine. The vertebra above has moved forward. This injury is usually due to high-velocity road accidents or falls from a height. It does not usually happen with just lifting a heavy load. Due to corresponding narrowing of the spinal canal and/or injury to the spinal cord, the patient can develop paralysis below the level of the injury.

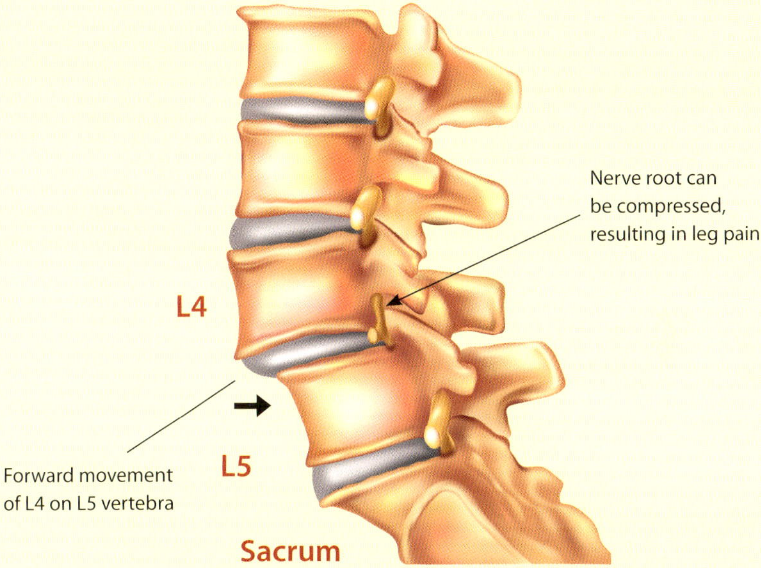

Diagram 4.11: Spondylolisthesis — A Forward Movement of One Vertebra on Another

The common cause of this slight abnormal movement of a vertebra over the vertebra below is due to a congential weakness of the spine (the part called the lamina). It can be a cause of back pain, especially after an activity like sports or heavy lifting.

In the diagram, the forward movement can result in the foramina (the opening through which the nerve leaves the spine) being narrowed. The patient may therefore also feel some pain going down the leg whenever there is irritation of the nerve root.

- **Instability:** Some patients have "instability" of the bones caused by weak ligaments secondary to disc degeneration or chronic stress on the back. Some movement of the vertebra may be noted.

Many patients who are labelled as "dislocation" or "out of alignment" are actually just suffering from an injury to the muscle, joints or cartilage of the spine. The injury causes a slight bend in the spine. It is not a true "dislocation".

The Facet Joints

There are joints, called facet joints, at the posterior (back) of the vertebral bones (Photo 4.12 and Diagram 4.13). These joints have smooth surfaces and have a bit of lubrication fluid inside to help movements. They are called synovial joints, like our finger joints.

So if we bend our spine forward, the discs in front will be compressed like a shock absorber, and the synovial joints behind slide forward.

> Ask a friend to stand in front of you and feel the bones at the lower spine. Make a mark with a pen. Then, ask him to bend forward. You will see that the spines move apart at the back as the facet joints allow the forward slide (Photo 4.14).

Why do facet joints cause pain?

Firstly, they can become stiff as we get older and do less stretching. We spend hours sitting or standing. The spine gets stiffer with time. If we suddenly bend over, we could experience pain or provoke an injury by suddenly stretching stiff joints.

Secondly, the joints develop osteoarthritis ("wear and tear") changes over the years. Older patients may feel backache from the worn out facet joints (Diagram 4.15).

The Soft Tissues (Spinous Ligaments and Connective Tissues)

The ligaments are the strong support tissues that surround and protect the spine discs and joints (Diagrams 4.16 and 4.17). There are many

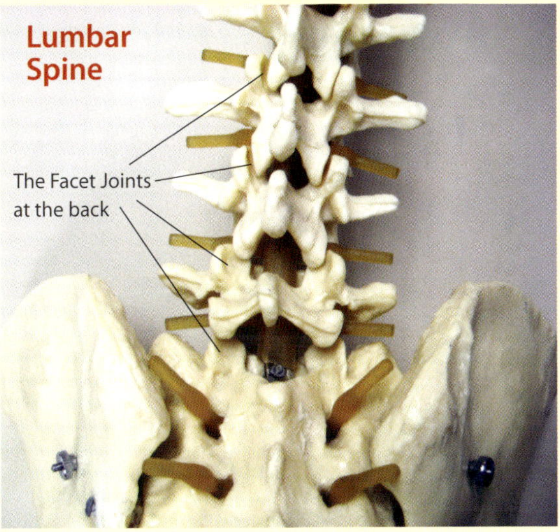

Photo 4.12: Model of the Spine
This model shows the facet joints clearly. The facet joints are at the back of the spine and allow for extension (backward bend) and flexion (forward bend) of the spine.

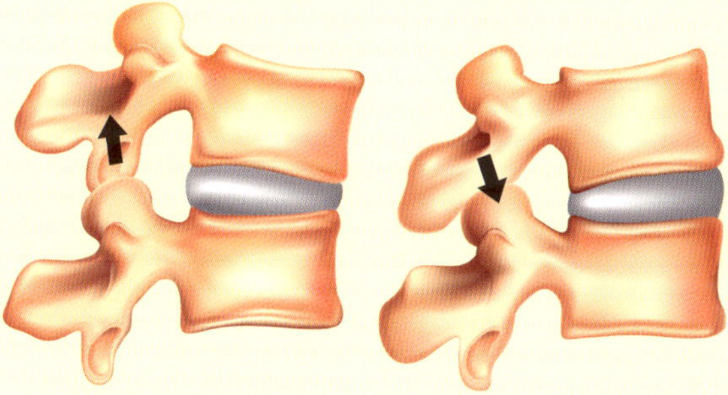

Diagram 4.13: Facet Joint Movements
The facet joints at the back of the spine are synovial joints. Synovial joints have smooth cartilage and allow movement. As seen in the diagram, the synovial joints move as the spine is extended backward or bent forward.

Degeneration and stiffness of the joints can cause pain. Maintaining flexibility in these joints helps protect against back problems.

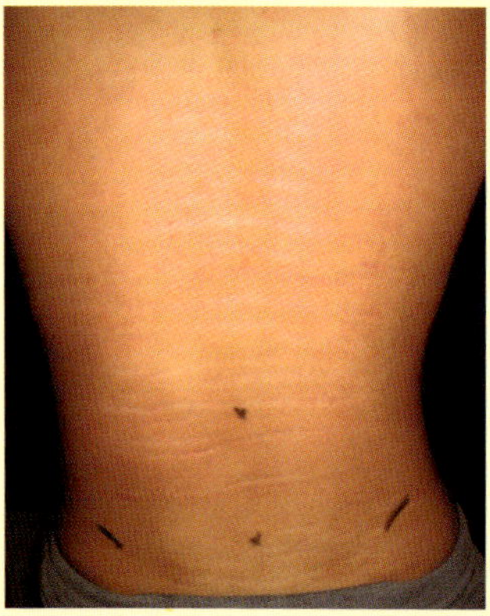

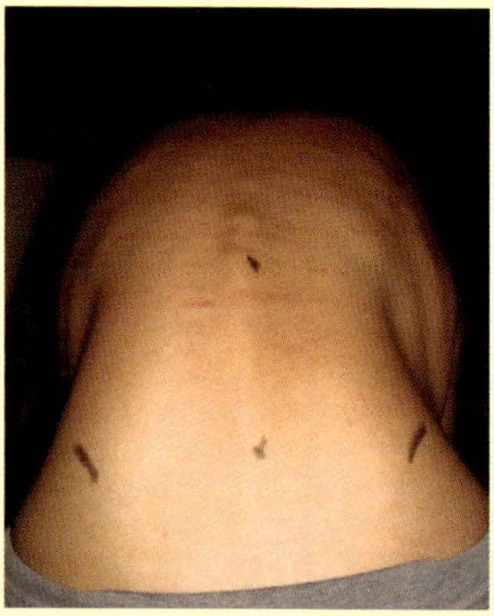

Photo 4.14: Flexibility of the Lower Spine

The photos show one of the simplest tests that can be used to look at spine flexibility. This young man has a flexible spine as noted by the separation of the marks placed on the skin while he bends over from a standing position.

Looking at the back, first standing and then bending forward, will give information about any curves, deformities, swellings, inflexibility and muscle wasting.

A flexible spine requires a healthy intervertebral disc ("the shock absorbers") and facet joints ("the sliders") as well as flexible spine ligaments.

Diagram 4.15: Facet Joint Osteoarthritis (Degeneration)

This diagram shows a degenerated facet joint, which loses the smooth cartilage and forms bone spurs. There is usually degeneration of the intervertebral discs as well.

Back pain can result from the osteoarthritis of the joints, which causes the bone to grind on bone. Leg pain can result from nerve root compression due to narrowing of the opening (foramen) caused by the bone spurs. The ligaments and soft tissues around the facets and vertebral body will also be weaker and contribute to chronic pain.

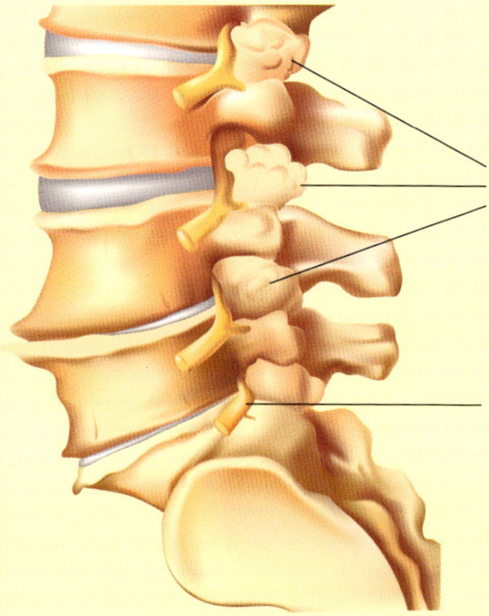

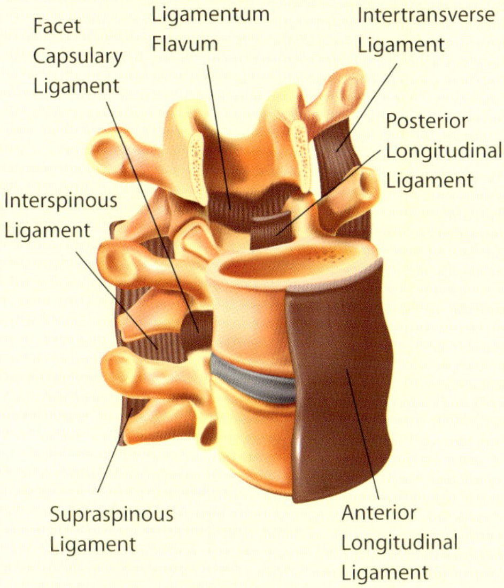

Diagram 4.16: Ligaments Supporting the Lumbar Spine

The ligaments above cover the vertebra anteriorly and posteriorly. The ligaments are support structures that prevent the vertebra from moving out of place. They prevent excessive bending and rotation of the spine. Ligaments can be weakened by age, the constant stress of lifting or sports, poor nutrition or an injury.

The ligaments that may be responsible for chronic back pain are: Supraspinous and Interspinous Ligaments, Intertransverse Ligaments and the Facet Capsule Ligaments.

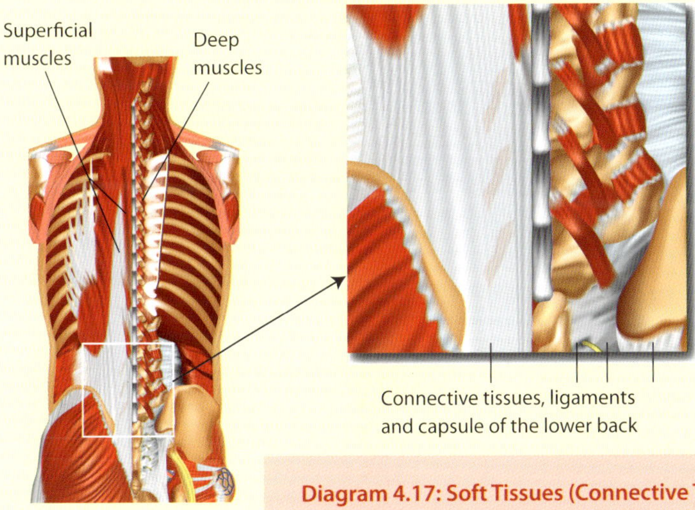

Diagram 4.17: Soft Tissues (Connective Tissues)

The white tissue covering of the muscles is the myofascial areas that can be a cause of back pain if they are weakened. Weakened fascia can be seen in many medical conditions (p.25) and stress-related issues (p.28).

supporting ligaments of the back that can be injured or be weakened over time, thus causing pain. Doctors may be able to tell which ligament is causing the pain by feeling the back and pressing deeply.

Recent ligament injuries behave like sprains. It could take six weeks or more for ligaments to heal after a fresh injury. Pain caused by chronic ligament weakness may need special treatments to help strengthen them.

The Muscles

Weakness of the spinal muscles is a major cause of chronic backache and of sudden attacks of severe back pain. Two main muscle groups contribute to the dynamic strength of the lower back (Diagrams 4.18 and 4.19). The abdomen (stomach) muscles help maintain spinal rigidity by increasing the support pressure in the abdomen (Diagram 4.20).

> Imagine a plastic soft drink bottle. When it is full of gas and under high pressure, the bottle is rigid and firm. When you open the bottle, the gas comes out and the bottle suddenly is soft and can be squeezed (Photo 4.21).

If the abdominal pressure is strong, patients will be protected from injury by a firmer spine. A weak abdominal muscle is a weaker spinal support.

The low back muscles are a group of muscles that stabilise the low back on either side of the spine. Strong back muscles help healing and also prevent the back pain from recurring.

The exercises to strengthen the back and abdominal muscles are very simple (see Chapters 14 and 15), and can take less than five minutes a day. All recent or chronic back pain and surgery patients are helped by these back strengthening exercises.

The Spinal Canal

The spinal canal is the space in which the nerves of the spinal cord are contained and protected. In older patients who have osteoarthritis, small bone spurs develop which reduce the space within the spinal canal

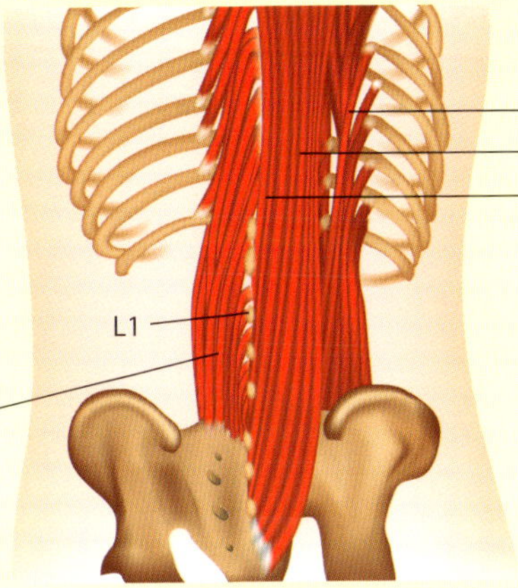

Diagram 4.18: Lumbar Spine Muscles (Multifidus and Erector Spinae)
The multifidus muscle is an important muscle for dynamic stability. For patients who develop chronic back pain, strengthening the multifidus muscle (and the others) reduces and even eliminates back pain. It is helpful to continue these exercises to prevent the recurrence of pain (p.115).

Abdominal Muscles

Important for supporting the spine

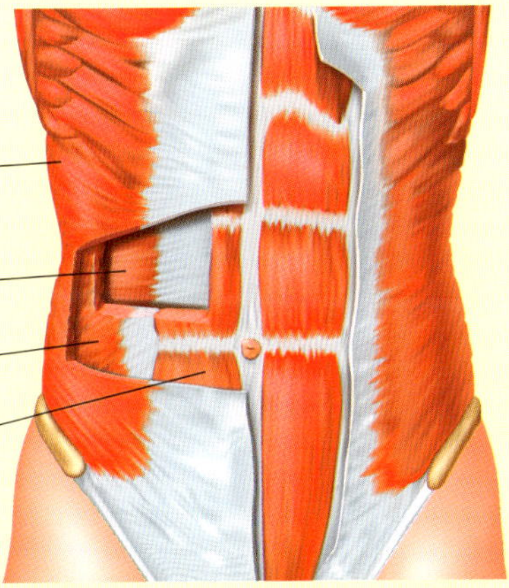

Diagram 4.19: Abdominal Muscles
The abdominal muscles help support the spine. This is especially true of the transversus abdominis, the deepest muscle. Specific exercises can strengthen the abdominal muscles and protect against back pain. For an explanation on how strong abdominals can protect the spine, see the main text (p.24, diagram 4.20 and photo 4.21).

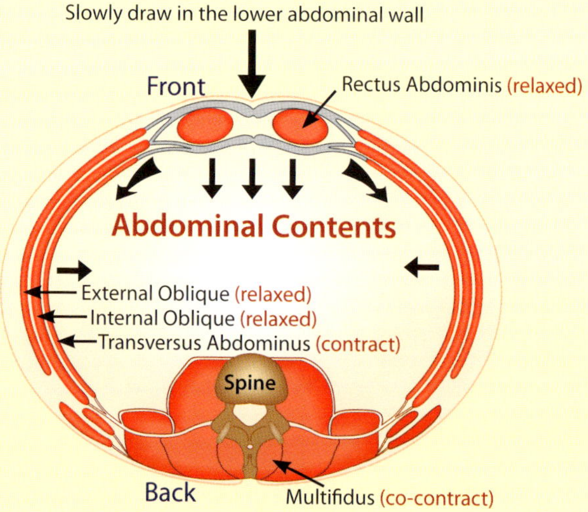

Diagram 4.20: Strong Abdominal Pressure
Strong abdominal muscles (specifically the Transversus Abdominis) will support the spine by increasing the intra-abdominal pressure. Just like an unopened bottle of cola keeps the plastic bottle firm, the firm abdominal muscles protect the spine. If pressure is low due to weak muscles, the spine is less supported (like an open plastic bottle of cola which has lost the carbon dioxide gas).

Photo 4.21: Rigid and Flaccid Plastic Bottle
This illustrates how pressure inside the bottle keeps the plastic walls firm. The unopened bottle cannot be compressed with pressure. Once the bottle is opened and compressed, the walls collapse inwards.

Similarly, strong abdominal pressure can raise the intra-abdominal pressure, and support the lower lumbar spine. Regular abdominal exercises protect against back pain.

(Diagram 4.22). The canal can be narrowed significantly and still not cause pain, revealing the adaptability of the nerves to a confined space. However, in some patients, the narrow canal causes nerve compression and they feel back pain, with pain in the buttocks and legs. This condition is called ***spinal stenosis***, and patients often complain that they cannot walk far, and that the pain is less when they sit down.

The Nerves

Compression on the nerve in the spinal canal or as the nerve comes out of the spine (through a canal called the intervertebral foramen) can cause pain (Diagram 4.23). The pain is typically described as radiating to the buttock and down the leg. Patients may feel numbness or paresthesia (pins and needles) along the leg. These are the symptoms associated with sciatica. It is important to remember that sciatica-like symptoms can be caused by problems outside the lower spine, so proper diagnosis is needed.

Other Causes

Other rare causes of damage to the bones causing pain are infections (e.g. pus) and tumours (e.g. cancer). Based on the history and other symptoms not related to the spine (e.g. weight loss, fever, cough), doctors may order tests to rule out these other causes of back pain.

General Health Problems

Apart for the low back structures, other medical conditions may cause or contribute to back pain. Some examples of general health issues are:

Diabetes

Patients who have poorly controlled diabetes have a greater incidence of backache and recover more slowly. Diabetes can cause the narrowing of the arteries. Just like clogged arteries to the heart can cause heart attacks in diabetics, clogged arteries to the spinal cord and spine can reduce the blood supply to the spine and nerves, and result in backache. Even

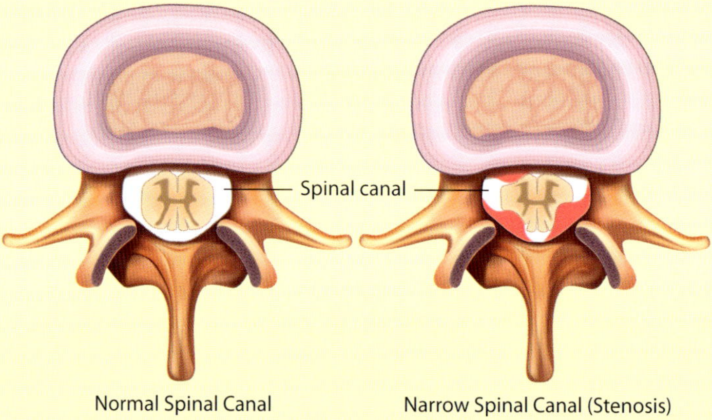

Diagram 4.22: Spinal Stenosis

Spinal stenosis refers to any condition that causes narrowing of the spinal canal, as shown in the diagram. The common causes of spinal stenosis are: osteoarthritis of the facet joints with bone spurs, protrusion of the disc or thickening of the ligaments supporting the spine (usually due to abnormal movements).

Spinal stenosis can cause backache due to the ligament and joint damage. Due to the narrowed spinal canal, spinal stenosis can give rise to leg pain and numbness because of nerve root compression.

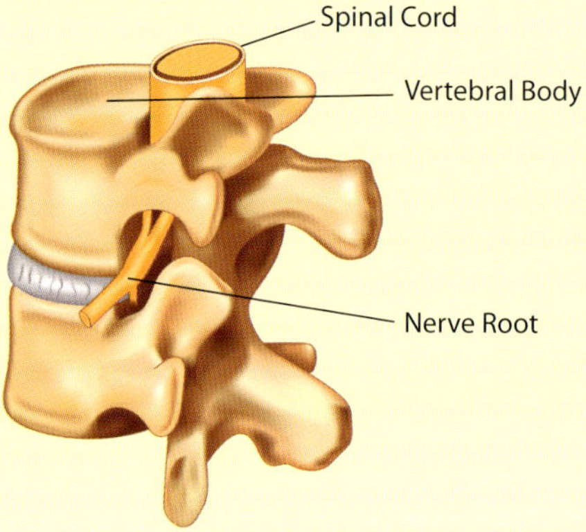

Diagram 4.23: The Spinal Nerves

The Spinal Cord runs in the spinal canal, and each spinal nerve root comes out at a different level. Note: If the spinal cord is compressed, all the nerves below will be affected leading to paralysis. If only one nerve root is compressed, then the pain is more localised.

healthy patients should reduce their intake of sugar by avoiding soft drinks and sugar in coffee or tea.

Gout

Gout is caused by the deposit of uric acid crystals in the covering of a joint. This causes swelling and inflammation. Inflammation in the facet joints of the spine can cause pain. Gout patients should avoid eating excessive meat or alcohol intake. Moderation in diet is a key to a healthy lifestyle and can protect against backache.

Vitamin Deficiency

Healthy spine bones and cartilage need an adequate intake of calcium and vitamins. Those who have backache can be helped by doses of vitamins B (B6 and B12), and also multivitamins and calcium supplements. Because it is difficult to know who does not have a balanced diet, multivitamins, calcium and vitamin B12 can supplement a normal healthy diet.

Lack of Water

Many people do not take enough water daily. Chronic dehydration can cause little cracks in the cartilage, which could contribute to backache. In a hot humid climate, at least 1.5 litres of water a day is needed to keep the body well hydrated.

Digestion and Constipation

Patients who have chronic bowel problems can suffer from backache, due to "referred" pain. "Referred" pain is where there is a problem in one organ but the brain senses the pain in another organ. Chronic constipation is a possible cause of chronic back pain.

Pregnancy, Menstruation and Birth Control

The monthly hormonal changes in women can have an effect on the lower back. In pregnancy, high female pregnancy hormones cause the weakening of ligaments and cartilage. This is the normal preparation for childbirth, but the side effect can be back pain due to weak back ligaments.

Many women complain of backache during menstruation. The hormonal changes involve similar hormones as pregnancy but not at the same high levels. Birth control pills may cause backache in the same way. Backache may lessen if the birth control pills are stopped.

Osteoporosis

This condition affects older people, especially women (see Chapter 11).

Stress-Related Problems

Stresses of Life

A study of back pain done among the workers in an aircraft factory found that workers unhappy or stressed out with their work seemed to get backache more often than others. Many other studies show similar results.

It is good for chronic low back pain sufferers to ask themselves the following questions:

- Is my job stressful (happy or not happy with work)?
- Has there been a change in my life recently (financial, social, marital)?
- Is there any change in home situation (e.g. new baby in the family, new home, relationship problems, loss of loved one)?
- Is my pain coming back whenever I get worried or stressed?

In the UK hospital I worked in, it was noted that the way a patient responded to stress affected their outcomes in surgery. All patients for surgery were screened and treated before surgery and personality tests were done. The result of surgery was better when stress was not contributing to the problem.

> I had two patients who had surgery on the same day for a spinal disc prolapse causing right leg pain and neurological signs. One

was a self-employed durian farm owner, the other was a financial advisor.

Both had the same operation (discectomy) and went home pain-free after a few days. Two weeks later, the farmer walked into my office pain-free. The financial advisor, however, came in a wheel chair. He complained that the pain had come back and he could not sleep. A repeat MRI scan showed that there was no disc protrusion or problem to account for the pain.

The difference between the two was that the officer was under a lot of stress, worried about getting "paralysed" and seemed reluctant to go back to work. The farmer was happy and already back to near normal activity.

Why does stress cause backache?

The **prolonged muscle tension** caused by stress can lead to back pain. For example, stress muscle tension can give headaches, neck pain and chest pain (like a heart attack). Many people do experience this type of temporary stress pain in their lives. For some, the pain becomes chronic.

Secondly, a person under stress will have a **higher level of stress hormones** like cortisol in the blood. These hormones can cause weakening and inflammation of soft tissues and ligaments. For example, stress inflammation can cause gastric ulcers or heart problems. It can also cause backache or worsen existing backache.

Learned Response (Coupled Response)

Non-related issues (e.g. job loss, family conflict) may have contributed by adding stress at the time of an episode of severe low back pain. The patient may have a relapse when the same psychological issue returns. The spine is healthy and there is no physical problem, but the patient will feel pain exactly like the first time. Chronic back pain patients have been shown in brain imaging scans to have increased activity in the emotion-regulating parts of the brain (prefrontal area).

Why does a learned response occur in some patients?

When the back is injured, a specific area in the brain records this information. If there is also an emotional stress like a job loss at the same time, then the brain seems to link this mental hurt to the same place. Months later, if the patient suddenly worries about a job loss, that area of the brain becomes active again and the patient feels severe backache.

The pain is real to the patient (not imagined) even though there is no problem with the spine. Learned response pain is very difficult to treat, and needs psychiatric treatment. The link between the injury and the psychological hurt/stress has to be broken.

Recent research using brain and spine scans suggests that nerves in the spinal cord that carry the pain sensations to the brain can develop cross-linkages (i.e. they get entangled) after an acute attack of back pain caused by an actual injury. This phenomenon (medically called "*neuronal plasticity*") essentially means that the nerves keep sending pain messages even after the original injury has healed completely. This is called "*neuropathic*" pain, and stress and emotional distress can aggravate the pain. Medications that can reduce neuropathic type pain are beginning to be used more frequently for chronic back pain.

5

The Tests for Low Back Pain

Low back pain is the non-specific complaint that brings you to the doctor. It is not a diagnosis. Doctors have to ask questions, do a physical examination and order various tests to find the cause of the back pain. Sometimes, patients have more than one problem affecting their back at the same time, and all these problems need to be understood and treated. Part of good treatment is to follow up with the patient to check the response, and to adjust the diagnosis and treatment. This is why it is not a good idea to keep changing doctors just because you feel you are not getting better quickly enough (Photo 5.1).

Patient's History of the Back Pain

Doctors will need accurate information about the back pain.

- *How did the pain start?* Backache can start suddenly (e.g. after sudden lifting or a fall) or slowly (sitting for long periods on a poorly designed chair or doing heavy work).

- *What caused the pain?* Did if you lift something, fall or twist the back? Did you change your footwear recently or buy a new bed? Did you encounter any recent problems in life (e.g. death of a close relative or relationship problems)?

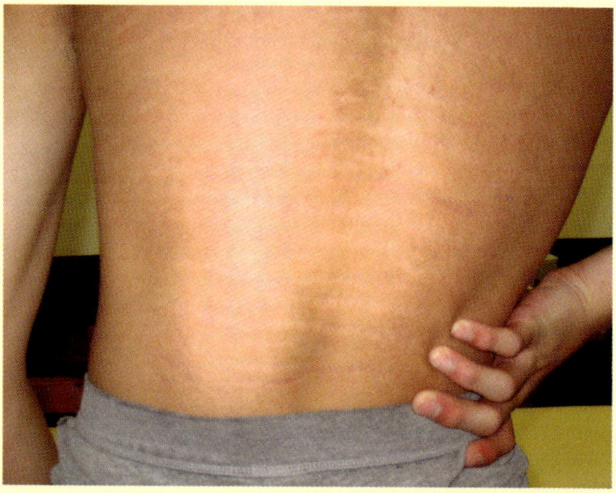

Photo 5.1: The Painful Back

Backache is not a diagnosis. It is a symptom or complaint that brings someone to see a doctor. There are many causes of back pain, but the complaint may be the same. So a patient holding his back and complaining of pain could have a disc tear or protrusion, a fracture, a back muscle tear, a muscle pull or a ligament injury.

To complicate matters, a patient holding his back this way may have kidney or ureteric stones, urinary infection, pancreatitis, gall stone, or possible intestinal problems like irritable bowel or infections. None of these is related to the lower back, so the doctor has to make sure that all these problems are excluded before offering treatment.

A proper diagnosis is essential to effective treatment.

- *How long have you had the pain?* If it is sudden or recent, we call it acute backache. If it lasts over six weeks, it is chronic backache. Recall if the pain is there all the time or just comes and goes.

- *What is the pain like?* (e.g. sharp pain, dull ache pain or pulling pain)

- *Does the pain move anywhere*? Does the pain go down the leg or into the buttock?

- *Is there any change in urine or bowel habits?* This is important for it can mean that the spinal cord nerves may be affected.

Physical Examination of the Patient

Physical examination reveals important information about the cause of back pain.

- **Curved or tilted spine**

If patient cannot stand straight or is tilted, it may be due to a muscle cramp (spasm). There may be a bend in the bone (Photo 5.2). This can be caused by scoliosis, osteoarthritis or an injury. A "step" may be felt and suggests a weak area in the spine causing some instability.

- **The exact point of the pain**

This can be found by applying direct pressure on the low back (centre and sides). There is often one place that is very painful to pressure (Photo 5.3). Tenderness in the centre suggests injury/problems with the disc or ligaments. Tenderness towards the sides or buttocks suggests facet joint pain or muscle cause.

- **Reduced movements of spine**

If the lower body cannot bend forward or backward, or rotate sideways, it could be an injury to the disc or muscle pain/spasm.

- **Unable to lift one leg higher than the other while lying down**

This may be because there is a nerve being pressed. You may feel the pain moving down the leg (Photo 5.4).

- **Weakness of the toes or foot**

The patient may experience weakness when bringing up the big toe or foot, or standing on his toes. This may suggest a nerve compression (Photo 5.5).

- **Changed sensation along the thigh, leg or foot**

There are "pins and needles" or "numbness" along some parts of the thigh, leg or foot. This may indicate a nerve compressed in the spine area (Photo 5.6).

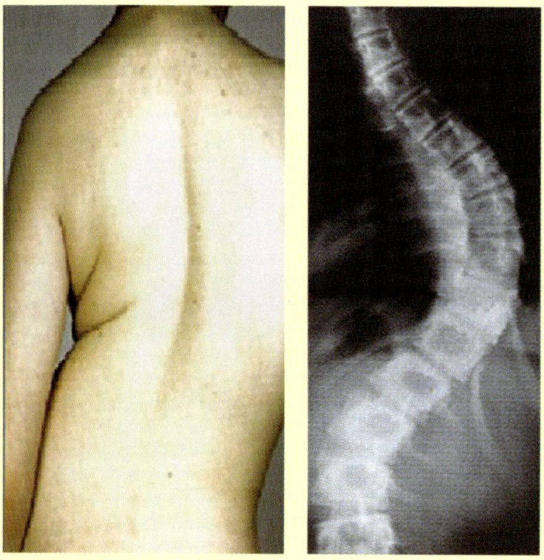

Photo 5.2: Curvature of the Spine (Most Cases are Milder Than This)

Scoliosis is a curvature of the spine that occurs in the teen years due to possible genetic causes. In rare cases, a predisposing disease may be identified and requires treatment. In general, if the curve is mild (less than 10 degrees), it is considered normal and no treatment is required.

Severe curves of over 40 degrees like this patient will need surgery to prevent back and lung/heart problems in the future. Patients in between need specialised scoliosis care.

Scoliosis in older persons can be due to degenerative changes in the spine, causing imbalance and malalignment. Patients who have osteoarthritis, with scoliosis, tend to be at greater risk of having chronic back pain.

During examination, we can assess the scoliosis and document the curve with X-rays. In the majority of patients, non-surgical methods of back pain treatment and flexibility/muscle strengthening exercises will help (refer to Chapter 4).

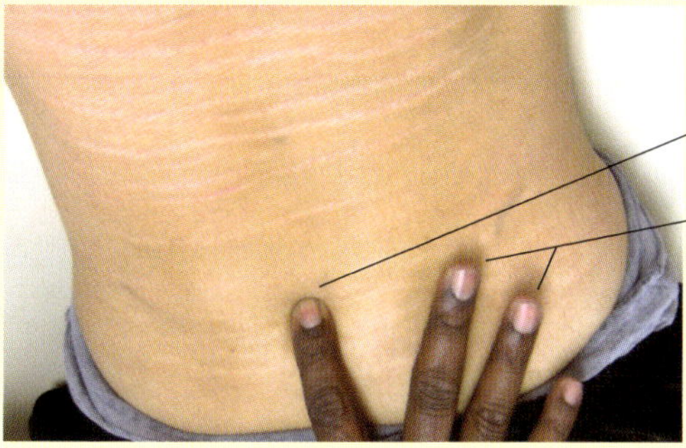

Photo 5.3: Palpation — Checking for Bone Deformity and Area of Pain

Palpation can reveal a lot about the back pain and rule out some of the other causes of backache. All the bony protuberances are felt to see if they are tender or if there is swelling. The common bony areas that can be palpated are the spinous processes and the pelvic bones. The muscles are then felt for painful nodules, spasm or swelling. Depending on the point of tenderness, some indication of the origin of the back pain can be made.

X-rays are done if there is suspicion of a bone problem. Muscle origin pain is usually treated initially without X-ray or other investigation.

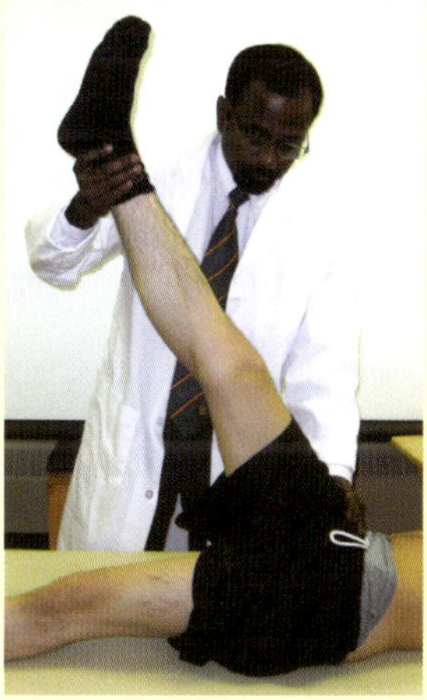

Normal Leg Raise

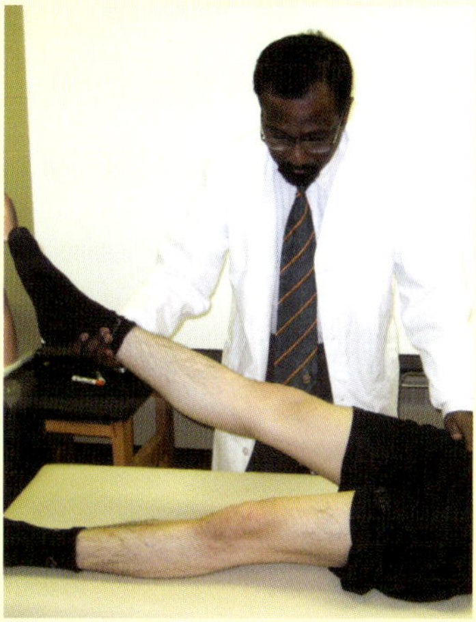

Restricted Leg Raise

Photo 5.4: Nerve Compression ("Pinched" Nerve)

This test helps the doctor to identify whether a nerve root that is coming out of the spinal column has been compressed. On the left is a normal leg raise test. The patient will feel no pain and feels tight at the extreme of the leg raise. On the right, the patient will complain of severe pain in his back radiating to his leg. The leg cannot be raised any further. This may indicate that the nerve is compressed in the spinal column or just as it exits the spine through the foramen. Leg raise can also be restricted in some muscle spasm and myofascial pain situations, so the expertise of the doctor is crucial to making the right diagnosis.

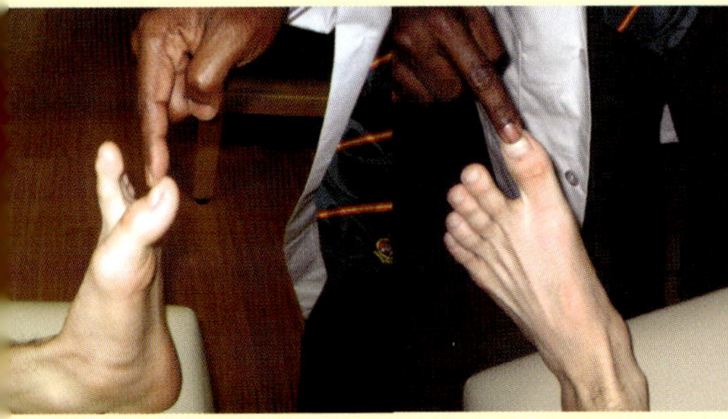

Weakness of the Left Big Toe
Can indicate a nerve compression due to a disc proplapse

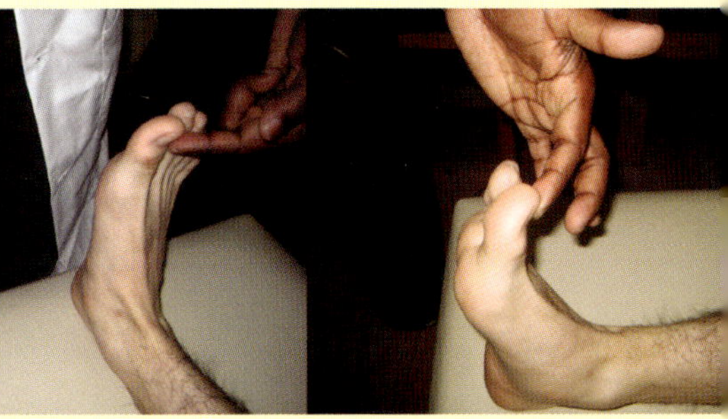

Normal Extension of the Big Toe
Indicates normal muscle power

Photo 5.5: Nerve Compression (Muscle Weakness)

If the compression on the nerves in the spine is severe, some of the nerve functions will be affected. There will be numbness and paresthesia (pins and needles sensation) felt in the leg. A more worrying sign is when there is mild weakness when extending the big toe. This is one of the common signs that doctors use to see if there is any significant nerve compression.

Note: This local weakness is not the same as paralysis. The patient can still walk around. It does not mean that urgent surgery is required. Very often, the compression is due to tissue inflammation and swelling, so with proper rest and treatment, the nerve compression will recover. In real paralysis, the patient will be weak in both lower limbs and is unable to walk; most, if not all, of his muscles are affected (hips, knees and ankles) and there is possible difficulty in passing urine or bowel motion.

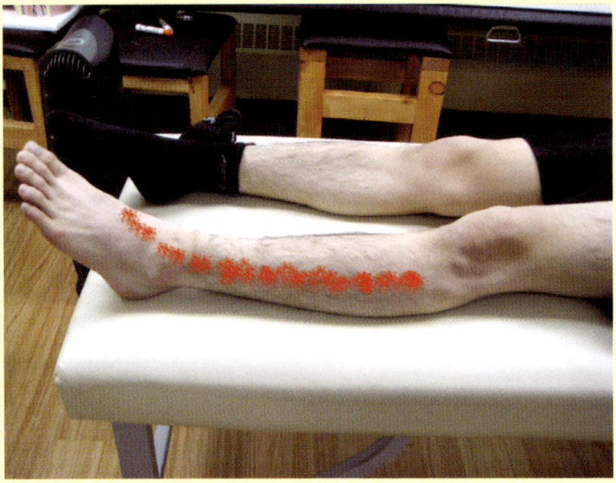

Photo 5.6: Numbness or Paresthesia ("Pins and Needles Sensation")

An example of the area where the patient may complain of numbness. Depending on the site of the numbness or reduced sensation, the doctor can deduce which nerve root may be compressed or inflamed. Numbness alone does not mean "paralysis" or an urgent operation.

Imaging Tests

- **X-ray**

An X-ray of the lower back is probably the most useful test to do for acute or chronic backache (Photo 5.7). Most of the time, this is the only screening test needed. X-rays are taken from the front and the side, and sometimes with the patient bent forward. Many of the bone, disc space and facet joint problems that cause back pain can be seen on X-rays.

- **CT (Computer Tomogram) Scan**

This test gives similar information as an MRI scan (Photos 5.8 and 5.9). It is usually done when simple treatments have not succeeded. It can be done if an infection, tumour or disc prolapse is suspected. It is not advisable for you, as a patient, to request a CT scan on your own.

- **MRI (Magnetic Resonance Imaging) Scan**

MRI shows soft tissues in even more detail than a CT scan (Photos 5.10 and 5.11). An MRI scan is done after you have been treated unsuccessfully for some weeks with simple and other non-operative treatments, *or if a more serious problem is suspected.*

Unfortunately, many first time patients have already done a scan before coming to a specialist, and they think that they need surgery. Many patients are fear being paralyzed. Even when told that they do not need surgery, the patient is already psychologically affected by the thought that he has a disc problem.

- **Myelogram**

In this test, a dye is injected into the space in the spinal canal and X-rays taken (Photo 5.12). It is an old test and is seldom done anymore because CT and MRI scans are available.

- **Ultrasound (Rehabilitative Ultrasound Imaging — RUSI)**

Ultrasound can check the size of the back muscles (e.g. multifidus) to look for wasting (smaller in size). If it shows small and unequal sized

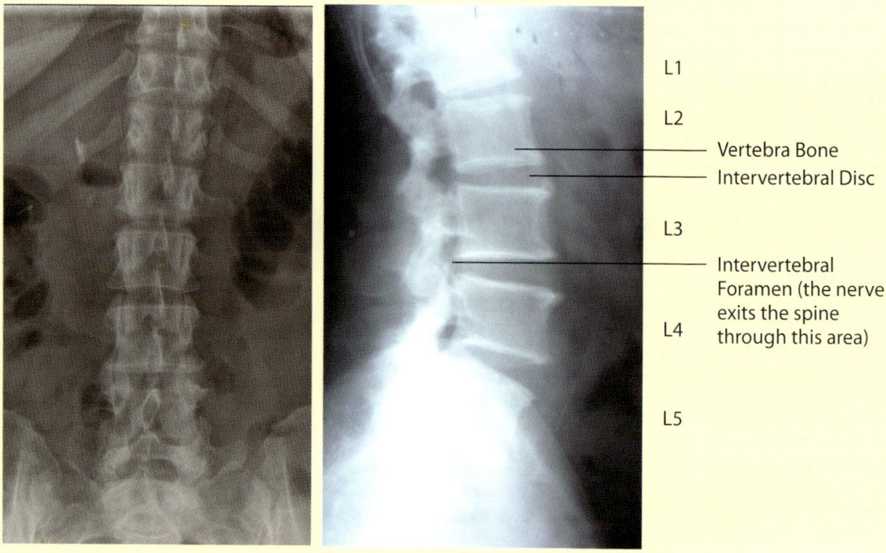

Photo 5.7: X-ray Appearance of Low Back (Lumbar Spine)

This is the basic and simplest investigation done for back pain. The bones are the most obvious structures seen clearly. Doctors will look for fracture or bone damage. The alignment will be assessed (for example, a muscle injury may cause spasm and a temporary straightening of the lumbar spine or a spondylolisthesis may be diagnosed).

The intervertebral disc is the space between the vertebral bones. While we cannot see the disc, we can see that the disc space is narrowed. That could indicate a damaged disc or degeneration.

The intervertebral foramen can be seen, as noted above. Any narrowing of the opening due to a bony cause can be seen on an X-ray. However, a protruded disc or soft tissue narrowing cannot be seen on normal X-rays.

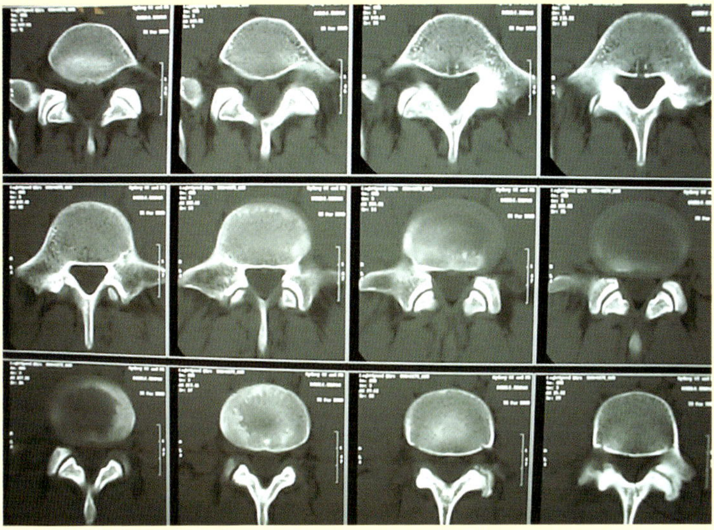

Photo 5.8: CT Scan

This is an example of a CT scan of the lumbar spine. It is usually viewed as a series of cuts (slices). Using the computer software, a side view can be created.

CT scans are not as clear as MRI for visualising the soft tissues and muscles, though it is sufficient to identify any disc prolapse which may need surgery.

Most doctors are likely to ask for an MRI and a CT scan for limited indications.

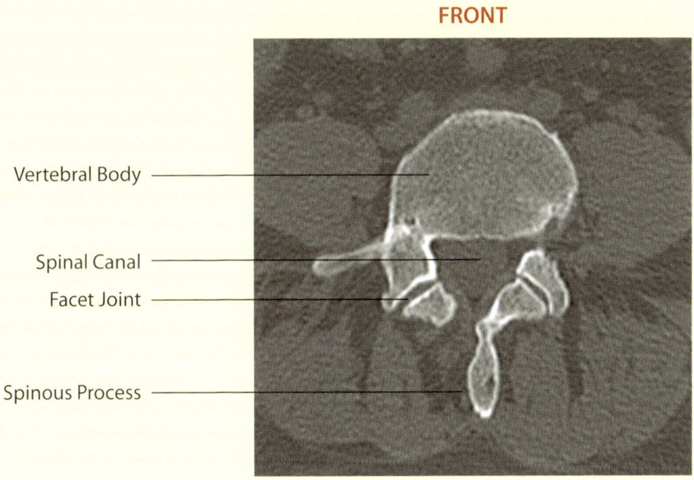

Photo 5.9: CT Scan of Spine (Top View)

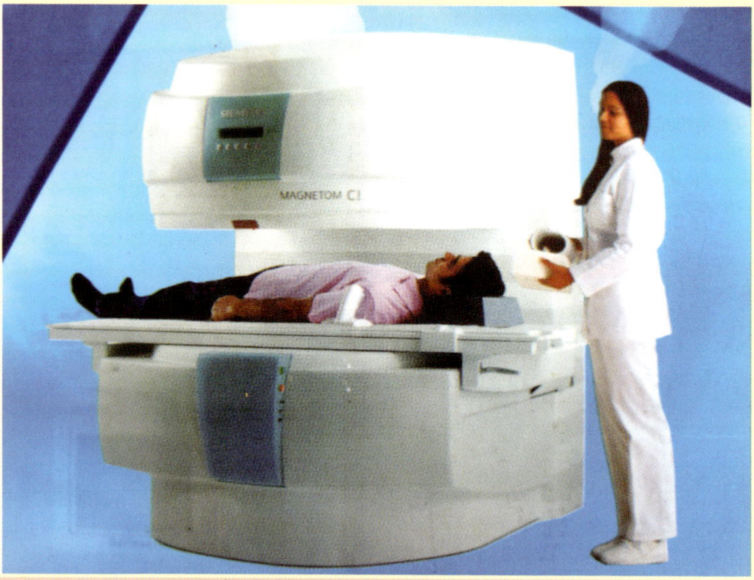

Photo 5.10: A Typical MRI Machine (MRI — Magnetic Resonance Imaging)

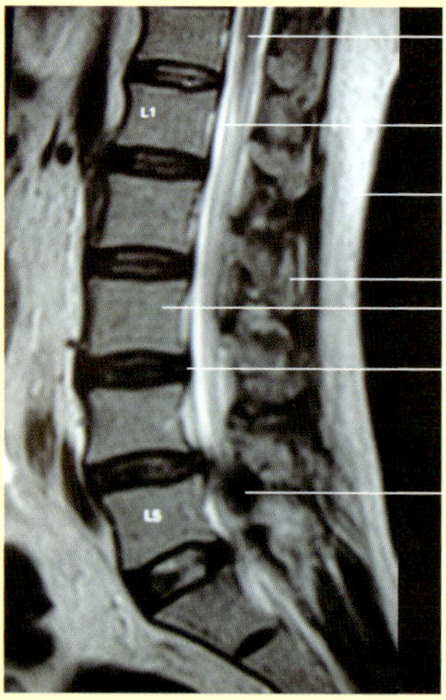

Photo 5.11: MRI Scan of Lumbar Spine — Prolapsed Intervertebral "Slipped" Disc

The MRI is usually the next investigation after an X-ray. It can show a number of structures as indicated in the scan above. Note the last disc space and the prolapsed disc. The white colour of the spinal canal is due to the signal caused by the fluid surrounding the spinal nerves.

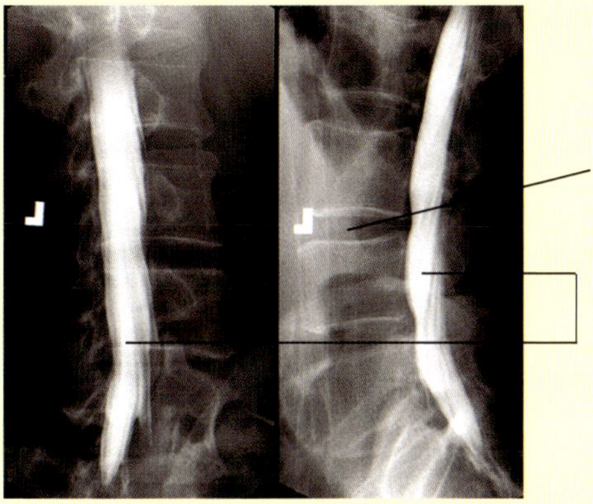

Photo 5.12: Myelogram of Lower Lumbar Spinal Canal
The myelogram was the commonest investigation done before the CT scan became available. For many years, the dye injected was oil-based, and remained in the canal for many years. Water-based dyes replaced oil-based dyes in the years before CT (the MRI) scans became the test of choice.

Patients who had myelograms with oil-based dyes in the 1970s and 1980s may get some back pain or leg pain from scarring around the nerves.

back muscles, back strengthening is needed. This test is only done in certain rehabilitation centres.

- **Bone Density Measurement**

Bone density measurement can be done using an ultrasound machine (Photo 5.13) or DEXA machines. This will tell if the spinal bones have osteoporosis.

- **3-D CT Scan**

These advanced scans use sophisticated computer programs to create a 3-D model of the bones. It is very precise in identifying the extent of bone injury, especially fractures (Photo 5.14). It is helpful to surgeons planning surgery. It is not widely available at present.

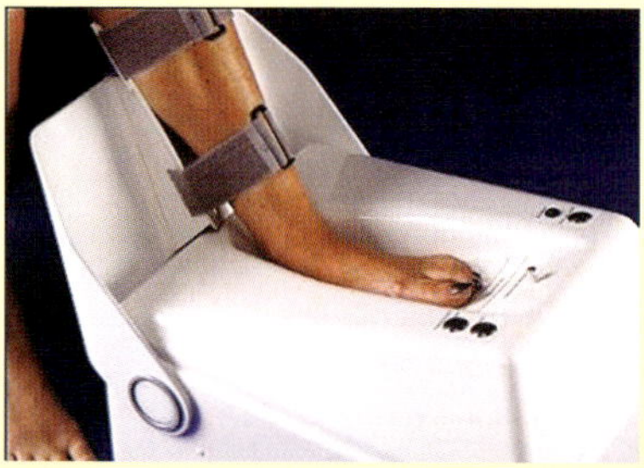

Photo 5.13: Simple Bone Density Measurement of Calcaneus Bone of Foot

This is a simple screening test that can be used inexpensively in a clinic setting to check for osteoporosis.

The test is based on the bone loss that may occur in the calcaneus bone. By using sound waves that pass through the bone, the density of the bone can be calculated.

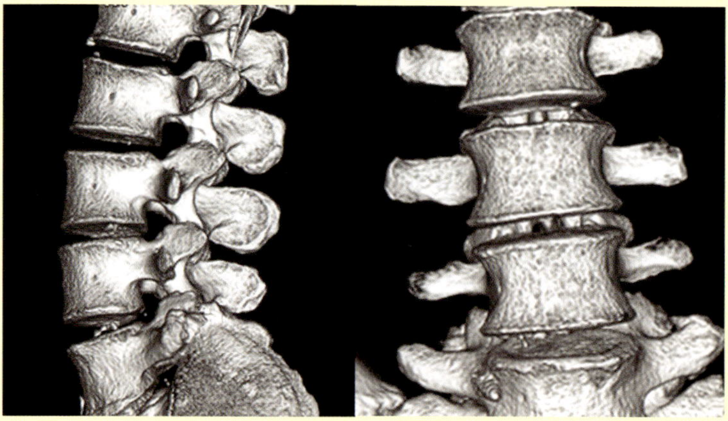

Photo 5.14: 3-D CT Scan

This is a specialised CT scan that uses X-rays and computer software to create 3-D images of the spine. The technology is likely to become more common with time. At present, MRI and regular CT scans are sufficient to diagnose and treat most of the common causes of back pain.

Section II

The Treatment of Low Back Pain

6

The Common and Routine Treatments

There are so many claims nowadays that you can get confused by the choices available. Many new on-operative treatments, devices and machines are aggressively advertised and promoted. After some time, the fad disappears and patients are left with costly beds, chairs, lamps or other equipment in their homes.

For patients with chronic back pain, life may be so difficult that they are willing to try anything. If a friend recommends a treatment, they are willing to try it. Some patients keep changing doctors, thinking that they do not recover after the first visit, the doctor is not good. Many patients try Western and traditional medicine at the same time!

The truth is that there are some established treatments that are proven by research to be effective. Generally, patients need a combination of treatments, and doctors need to monitor and adjust the treatment over time.

Treatments are basically grouped into the following categories:

1. Initial Treatments
2. Non-Surgical Treatments
3. Surgical Treatments
4. Preventive Measures

Most sudden backaches recover with rest and simple treatments. If in doubt or if the pain is severe, not getting less or affecting your work, you should see a doctor.

Initial Treatment Protocols For Low Back Pain

This approach is used for all back pain patients, especially when the pain is acute.

- **Bed Rest**

Patients are advised bed rest for severe low back pain, but only for a short time. Staying in bed for too long is bad for the spine — it weakens the muscles and causes the disc pressure to increase.

I advise patients to get up as soon as they can, depending on how much pain they can tolerate. I encourage patients to go back to work as soon a possible. If you do heavy work and need medical leave, I would still advise you not to stay in bed but to walk around the house and go for slow walks.

- **Hard Bed**

For a long time, the standard advice for back pain has been to lie on a hard bed or the floor. Lying on the floor may actually cause more pain. The approach today is to lie in whatever position you are comfortable with. You can use a moderately firm mattress rather than a hard floor. A pillow under the knees when lying flat or between the legs when lying on the side reduces the pressure on the lower spine (Diagram 6.1 and Photo 6.2).

- **Straight Chair**

You can sit anyway you want as long as you are comfortable and the pain is manageable. After every half hour, you should stand up and relax for about a minute. This reduces stress on the spine. Pressure measurements show that the pressure in your spine discs is lower when you stand than when you sit.

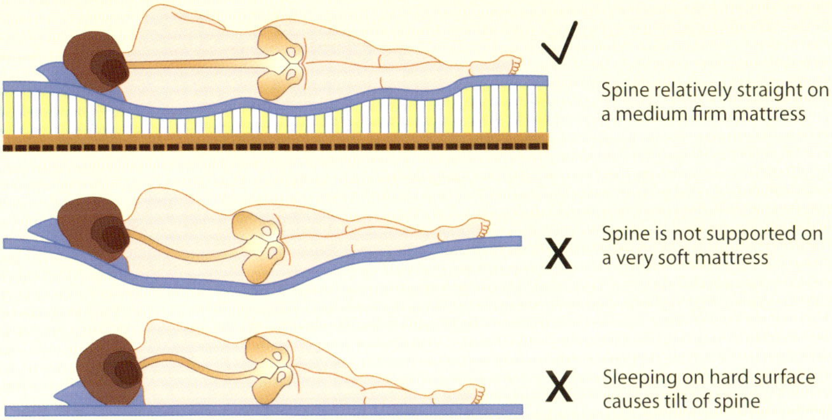

Diagram 6.1: A Moderately Firm Bed is Best for Back Pain

The goal of a mattress is simple. The patient needs to be comfortable and have a good sleep without waking up with back pain. The mattress must also give some support to the spine as indicated in the diagram.

The diagram of the spine shows why it is not recommended nowadays to sleep on the hard floor but to find a moderately firm mattress.

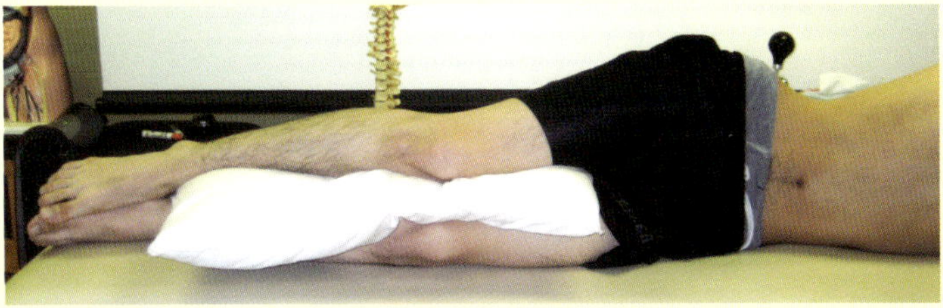

Recommendation 1: If you are lying on the side, place a pillow between the legs.

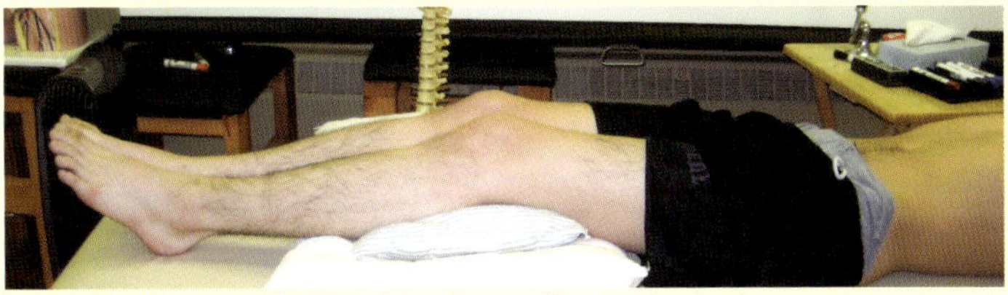

Recommendation 2: If you are lying flat, a pillow under the knees relaxes the spine and avoids excessive bending (lordosis).

Photo 6.2: Sleeping Position — Pillows

Using a pillow to get a better spinal position while sleeping is a good idea. There are two main recommendations, based on whether you are sleeping on your side or on your back.

- **Painkillers**

If the pain is sudden and severe, it is not necessary to suffer in pain. Simple painkillers can be helpful in the first few days. Once the pain is reduced, all you may need are some anti-inflammatory medicine (NSAID) for about a week. If you have gastric problems, antacids can be given. Painkillers are available as tablets or injections.

- **Anti-Inflammatory Medicines**

Non-steroidal anti-inflammatory medicines (NSAIDs) help reduce swelling (inflammation) of the spine tissues. NSAIDs can help reduce pain, which is a good side benefit. NSAIDs may cause gastric pain and bleeding. To avoid these problems, doctors usually give gastric medication with anti-inflammatory medicines. Some newer medications have less of such side effects and you may be given these medicines if you have prior gastric problems.

- **Muscle Relaxant Pills**

Muscle tension and spasm can cause backache and/or contribute to the pain. Muscle relaxant pills are used if the spinal muscles are noted to be cramped and painful, thus causing back pain.

- **Nerve Pills**

Higher doses of vitamins B6 and B12 are used as "nerve" strengthening vitamins. These vitamins do help neurogenic (nerve type) pain recover faster. It is effective if the back pain is associated with pain moving down the leg.

- **Multivitamins and Minerals**

Many patients with back pain may not know if they lack certain vitamins or minerals in their diet, contributing to prolonging their pain. Multivitamin and calcium supplements help the healing process. If you are older or have bone weakness (e.g. osteoporosis), then vitamin D supplements are added.

- **Glucosamine**

Glucosamine is a common alternative medicine. It helps in cartilage protection and is useful for "wear and tear" (osteoarthritis). It may also help in pain relief. There are minimal side effects and many of my patients now take these supplements regularly.

- **GABA Analogues**

The GABA analogues were initially introduced as a treatment for epilepsy. However, recent medical studies show they are effective for pain relief, particularly chronic neuropathic pain. In simple terms, neuropathic pain is pain that continues to be felt even after the original injury has healed. The GABA analogues prevent new nerve connections that cause these "false" signals to be perceived by the brain.

- **SSRI or SNRI Medications**

These medications were usually used as anti-stress medications but now have been shown to reduce chronic low back pain. Large-scale studies have confirmed their effectiveness and the US drug agency (FDA) has approved the use of these medications after extensive multi-centre studies.

Note

GABA analogues and SSRI/SNRI medications must be taken after proper assessment by a doctor.

7

Non-Surgical Treatments

Physiotherapy

Physiotherapy is an important second line treatment for backache. Most of the treatments help reduce the pain while the spinal tissues are healing. Commonly used physiotherapy methods are:

Cold Packs

Cold packs are useful for recent injuries or acute pain. It reduces the swelling (inflammation) that comes after an injury and lessens the bleeding in the area. By keeping the swelling down, it reduces the pain (Photo 7.1).

Hot Packs — Superficial Heat Therapy

Hot packs or thermal pads can be applied over the painful area, giving temporary pain relief. An infra red lamp does the same thing but is more expensive. Superficial heating of the skin works by increasing the blood flow, bringing more nutrients to the area. It also helps tight tissues to become more relaxed. Unfortunately, the heat does not go very deep under the skin. It is useful for osteoarthritis, and for the ligament and muscle pains (Diagrams 7.2 and 7.3).

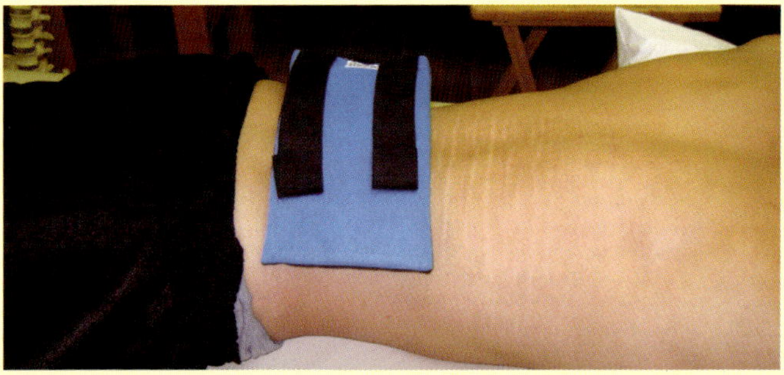

Photo 7.1: Application of Hot or Cold Treatment (Applied over the Painful Area)

The above pack can be used cold (from the fridge) or hot (soaked in hot water). There are many similar products in the market that you can buy.

Alternatively, you can use a simple folded towel (taken from the fridge for cold treatment or soaked in hot water for hot treatment).

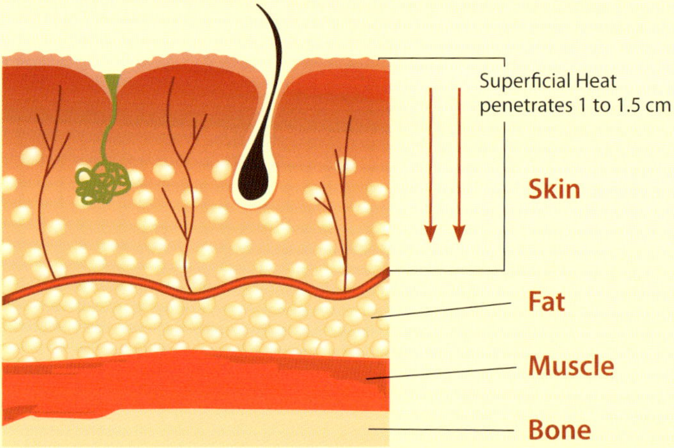

Diagram 7.2: Superficial Heat/Cold Therapy

In superficial heat or cold therapy, heat is transmitted through the skin by direct conduction of heat/cold. Thus, if the heat is too much, the skin will burn.

The most comfortable heat (e.g. infra red lamp or hot towels) can penetrate up to one centimetre only.

The heat thus does not reach the bone nor, very often, the muscles.

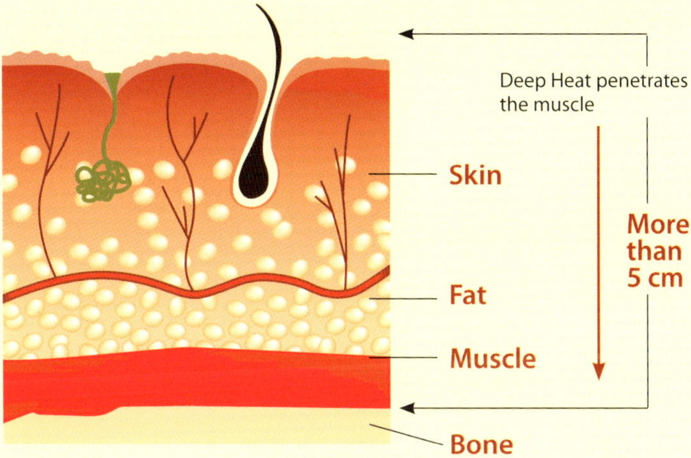

Diagram 7.3: Deep Heat Therapy (e.g. Ultrasound, Short Wave, Microwave)

Deep heat usually requires some equipment in a physiotherapy clinic. The trick is to heat up the muscle and deeper tissues without burning the skin.

Ultrasound, short wave, microwave and deep interferential currents (using a TENS like machine) can provide this therapy.

Tissues respond to the increased blood supply, and the nutrients and healing cells that are brought to the area.

Deep Heat

Deep heat uses various ways of increasing the heat in the deep tissues since superficial heat does not penetrate more than a few millimeters under the skin. By increasing the blood supply to the deep areas, nutrients and repair tissues can heal the structures which cause the pain.

- ***Ultrasound*** (sound waves)

Ultrasound uses sound waves that are targeted at the damaged and painful and deep tissues. It can be used for small areas of maximum pain (Photo 7.4).

- ***Short Wave Diathermy*** (high frequency electrical current)

High frequency electrical currents are used to stimulate currents in

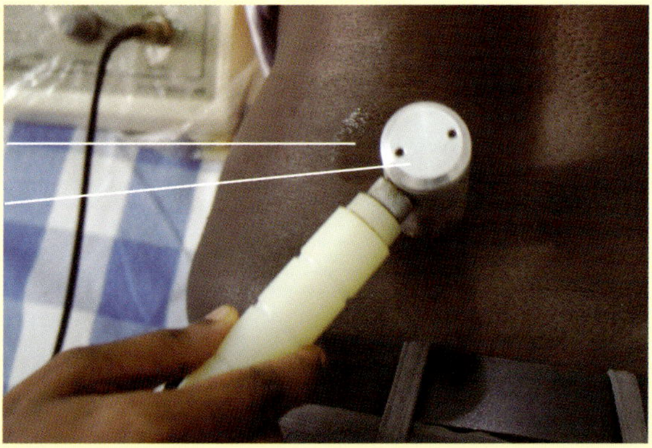

Photo 7.4: Ultrasound
The ultrasound waves are emitted through a transducer. A gel is used to facilitate good transmission of the sound waves from the transducer to the skin.

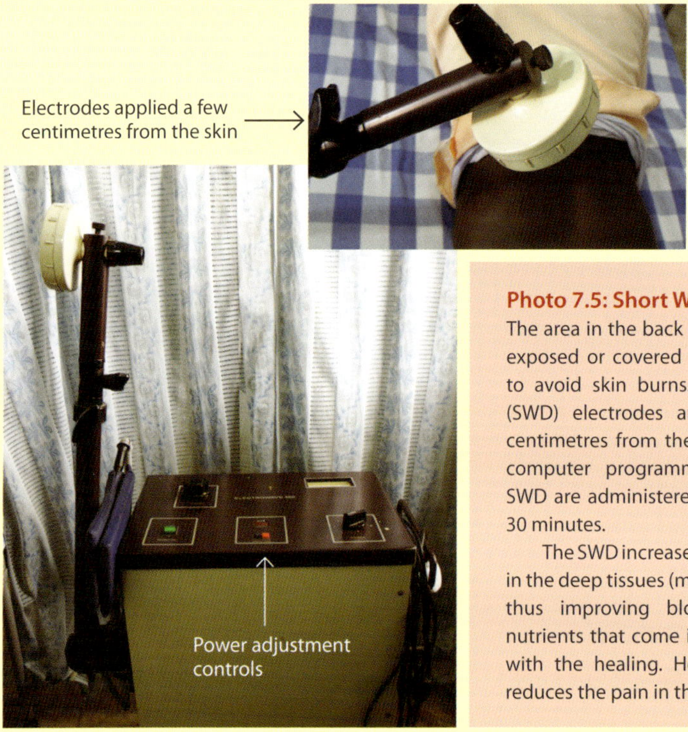

Photo 7.5: Short Wave Diathermy
The area in the back which is painful is exposed or covered with a light cloth to avoid skin burns. The short wave (SWD) electrodes are placed a few centimetres from the skin and certain computer programmed amounts of SWD are administered for about 15 to 30 minutes.

The SWD increases the temperature in the deep tissues (muscles and fascia), thus improving blood supply. The nutrients that come into the area help with the healing. Heat by itself also reduces the pain in the area.

the deep tissues, thus heating the deep areas. This method is better for a large area heating (Photo 7.5).

- *Microwave Therapy* (electromagnetic waves)

This method is also suitable for larger areas. It uses electromagnetic energy to stimulate the deep tissues, with an effect similar to Short Wave Diathermy.

Low Level Laser Therapy (LLLT)

This technique directs a beam of laser light into the injured area. The skin does not feel anything and no heat is generated in the deep tissues. Healing seems to occur by increasing blood supply and stimulating the body's own repair process (Photo 7.6). It is an option to be considered as an alternative to deep heat.

Pelvic Traction

This involves pulling the lower spine using either manual weights or a traction device. It works by stretching the cramped and painful muscles, making them relax (Photo 7.7). It does not help a disc protrusion to go back into place. Some patients go for traction even for chronic pain. While they feel better temporarily, there are less obvious long term benefits.

TENS (Transcutaneous Electrical Nerve Stimulation)

This device applies a current to the skin using pads on the skin. Many TENS machines are now available for patients to use at home. It works by interfering with the perception of pain by the local nerves. TENS can reduce the pain of recurrent backache. It reduces the need for pain-killing medicines (Photo 7.8).

Muscle Electrical Stimulation

Using stronger current in a clinical setting, certain back muscles can be made to contract and relax. This can strengthen these weak back muscles.

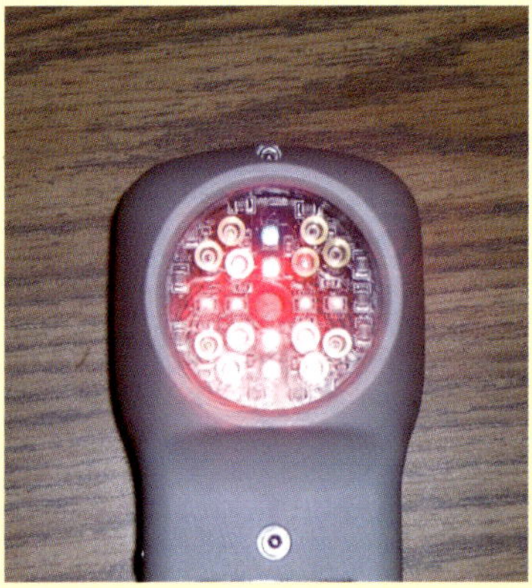

Photo 7.6: Low Level Laser Light Probe

The laser light (low intensity) is emitted through multiple sources. Smaller probes are available. The light is directed into the area which is painful. The light energy (photons) is absorbed by the damaged cells and this stimulates the cells to increase production of healing proteins. By increasing the healing process in the injured area, the pain slowly diminishes.

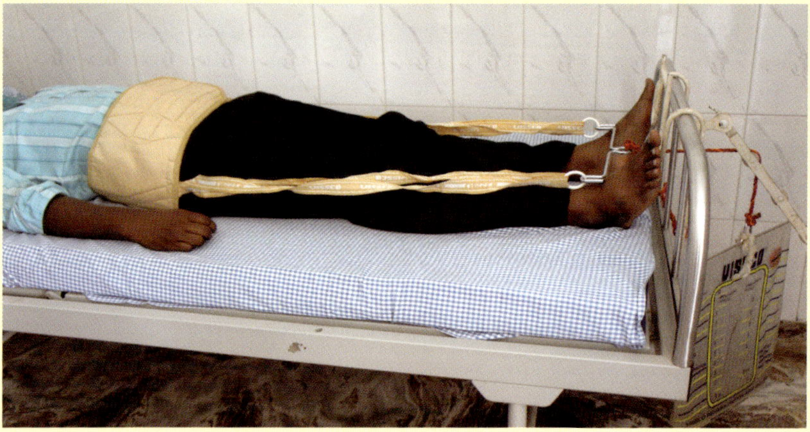

Photo 7.7: Pelvic Traction in the Ward

This is a common method that has been used for many years. If the patient is in severe pain and admitted to hospital, a pelvic belt is strapped around his waist. A plastic bag with water acts as weight, and is hung from the end of the bed. By adding or removing water, the weight can be adjusted to suit the patient's comfort.

While we used this technique for two to six weeks in the past, studies show that it is not wise to stay in bed that long. Pelvic traction may be used if pain is severe, and it is removed once the patient is comfortable and can stand up.

Electrode pads placed on the skin

Photo 7.8: TENS (Transcutaneous Electrical Nerve Stimulation)
The pads are attached to the skin with tape. Gel is applied between the pad and the skin to facilitate the electrical conduction.

The pads are attached to a TENS machine, which can be programmed to pass a certain amount of electrical impulses through the skin. Very strong impulses can cause muscles to contract.

Back Strengthening Exercises

These exercises can be done under the supervision of a physiotherapist. The patient can learn the exercises and do them at home.

Back Stretching and Flexibility

Here, the therapist helps to improve the movements of the spine and hips. This loosens tight tissues and helps reduce pain. Patients can practise this at home.

Spinal Decompression

A new variation of traction is becoming popular because of intensive advertising in the newspapers and television. These machines claim to be able to exert a strong pull on the lower spine, even pulling "slipped" discs into place. Medical studies so far do not support significant benefits from spinal decompression as compared to regular traction (Photo 7.9).

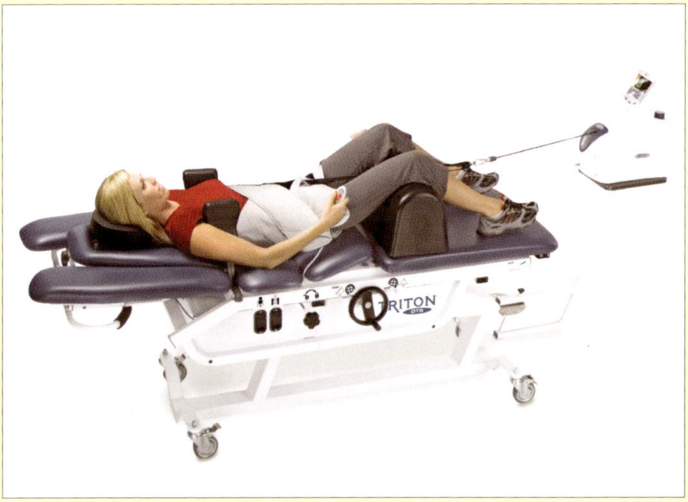

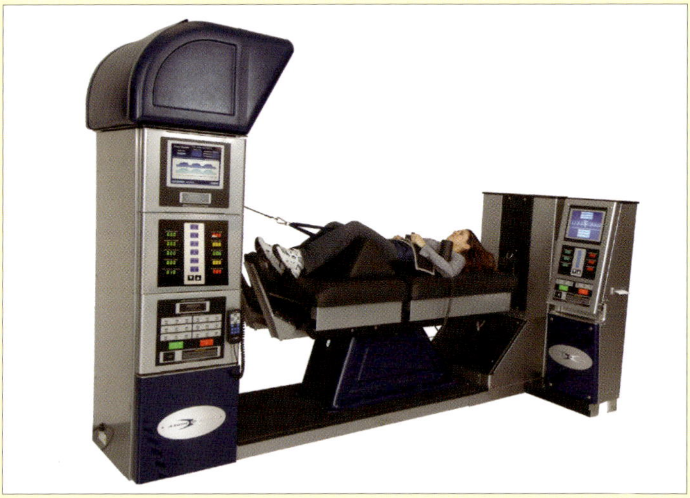

Photo 7.9: Spinal Decompression (Traction)

Recently, many spinal decompression centres offer a new form of what is basically traction teatment. Machines like these are becoming popular and do help reduce intensity of back pain. The machines, and therefore the costs of treatment, can be expensive, thus not everyone can afford it.

However, the claims to be able to heal a prolapsed disc have not been firmly proven by evidence-based clinical trials yet. Notice the similarity to the simple and cheaper traction method (see Photo 7.7), which can be done at home.

Manipulation

Manipulations help when the pain is caused by joint or ligament tightness (Photo 7.10). By loosening tight tissues and breaking up tight trigger areas, flexibility is improved and the pain diminishes. Manual therapists may use slow, gentle pressure. Chiropractors may apply quick and more direct force. Many traditional medicine methods (e.g. "urut" or native massage) may use a combination of sudden force, gentle manipulation and massage. Massage techniques can help relax tight muscles, increase blood supply to the area and break up tight tissues around joints. Whatever the method used, patients do get temporary relief if they go to an experienced practitioner of these alternative treatments.

Sometimes, patients misunderstand the meaning of terms which are used by doctors and alternative medicine.

> For example, many patients are told a manipulation is needed because the spine is "dislocated" or "out of place". From a medical view, it is more likely a stiff joint that needs a release. For a doctor, a real dislocation of the spine is a serious injury, and manipulation should not be done. Sometimes, a sound may be heard when "manipulations" are done. This "pop" sound is due to a vacuum effect created in the facet joints. It is the same as the sound you get when you crack your finger joints, not a sign that your bone is out of place or going into place.

Orthopaedic surgeons can do lower spine manipulations under a general anaesthetic. It is uncommon now, mainly because patients are afraid of anaesthesia and it requires admission to hospital. Also, there is now the effective use of direct manipulative methods and/or orthopaedic injection techniques.

Acupuncture

Acupuncture has gained prominence over the last few decades in the treatment of chronic and acute low back pain. The mechanism of how

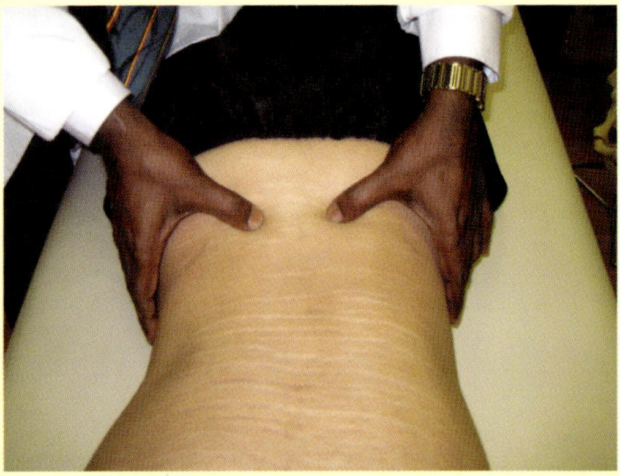

Facet Joints of L4-L5 vertebral level

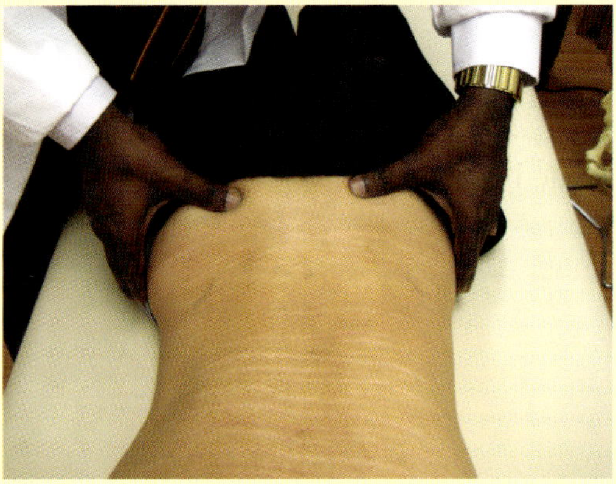

Sacro-iliac joints

Photo 7.10: Manipulative Techniques

The therapist identifies the deep and tender muscle nodules and, with gentle but firm pressure, will "roll" the nodule and "knead" it till it becomes softer and less sensitive. Regular soft tissue manipulation brings pain relief after some time, but this treatment requires regular visits to the clinic. Massage therapists, soft tissue manipulative therapists and many chiropractors and osteopaths are using this technique with great effect.

acupuncture actually works is not scientifically known yet and research is ongoing.

Some patients get good pain relief with acupuncture. Repeat treatment is needed as the effects are often temporary. Treatments can range from use of needles with or without a small electric current. The effect can be similar to physiotherapy with superficial current (TENS). Some acupuncturists use pressure on the acupuncture points, without needles, for patients who fear being pricked.

Relaxation Techniques and Biofeedback Therapy

Muscle tension and tightness are an important component of back pain. This technique trains patients to consciously relax the tensed muscles by measuring electric impulses in the painful muscles (electromyography). Good pain relief is possible but it takes many hours to learn this technique. Many patients do not have the patience to follow through.

Stress Relief and Anti-depressant Treatment

Patients who have chronic back pain (pain lasting over three months) experience increased stress and depression. Chronic pain can persist long after the original back injury or disc problem has healed. It is a cycle that needs to be broken because pain can cause depression, and depression then causes more pain.

Medical research and brain scan imaging are proving that the mind-body connection causing back pain is real. The pain is not imagined. There are simple anti-depressants available today that have minimal side effects and are effective in most chronic back pain patients.

8

Specialised Non-Surgical Treatments

Trigger Point Treatments for Low Back Pain

Fibromyalgia or Myofascial Pain Syndrome

Despite the regular treatments described so far, there are patients who have seen many doctors, taken many pills, tried all kinds to alternative treatments and bought all kinds of devices, and yet continue to have back pain. Patients tend to feel that nothing is helping them and often become depressed. These types of chronic back pain symptoms have no obvious bone or cartilage/disc problems on X-ray or MRI scans.

What are Trigger Points?

In most of these patients, the pain is caused by painful muscles, which feel like hard tender lumps (nodules) called "trigger points". This muscle backache can mimic a slipped disc or back injury. Patients improve if the "trigger points" can be made less painful. This non-specific cause of back pain is variously called **Fibromyalgia** or **Myofascial Pain Syndrome**. The painful trigger points of fibromyalgia or myofascial pain syndrome can be treated in several ways:

- *Massage Therapy and Manipulation*

The trigger points are massaged deeply to "break up" the painful muscle lumps (Photo 7.10). It can be very painful, depending on the force used by the therapist. Pain relief is good but temporary, thus requiring the patient to be treated regularly for weeks or months. Alternative medicine techniques like "urut", ethnic massage, acupressure or shiatsu massage probably work in this way. Some patients have been on treatment for years.

- ***Physiotherapy***

Various physiotherapy techniques can be used to relax and break up the "trigger points". We can use ultrasound, short wave diathermy, low level laser therapy or similar techniques. They work by relaxing muscle tissue and reducing the pressure in the "trigger point" lumps.

Trigger Point Injection

Painful trigger point nodules in myofascial pain syndrome can be more easily treated and with long lasting relief by direct injection. Injection is effective for patients *whose pain has not improved* after all the other therapies.

The most common injection used is a combination short and long acting local anaesthetic, with a small dose of triamcinolone (a non-soluble steroid) or its derivative. The diluted local anaesthetic will help numb, soften and inactivate the nodules, giving early pain relief. The triamcinolone will reduce the inflammation and give longer lasting pain relief.

More recently, orthopaedic surgeons have begun using **botox** injections into the trigger zones. Botox has the same effect in inactivating trigger points as local anaesthetic and triamcinolone, but is much more costly.

The common areas in the low back where trigger points are injected are shown in the diagram (Photos 8.1, 8.2 and 8.3. Also, see the chart in Chapter 16). The long term results are very good, especially in treating chronic pain. To prevent recurrence, muscle strengthening and back stretching must be continued.

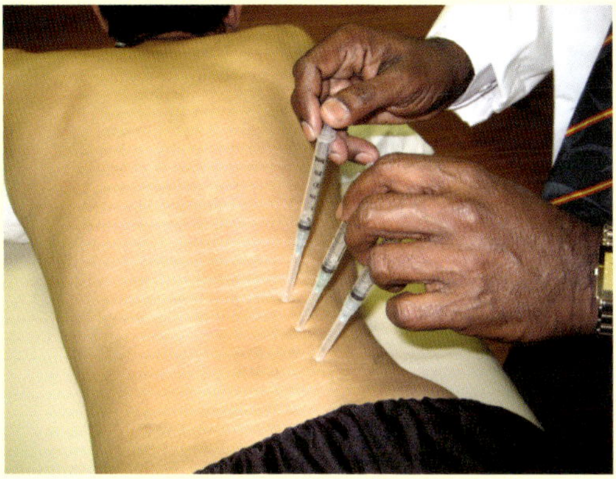

Photo 8.1: Example of Trigger Point Injection Sites

This is an example of how we determine which sites to inject. In trigger point therapy for myofascial pain and painful muscle trigger zones, direct injection yields much faster results than traditional massage therapy or soft tissue manipulation therapy.

By using small needles, the patient does not feel much discomfort. The local anaesthetic in the mixture helps numb any soreness that may be felt after the injection, and brings quick and immediate relief of pain.

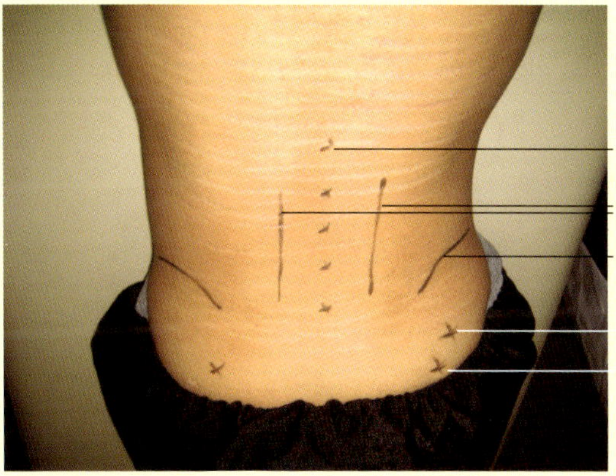

Photo 8.2: Sites Usually Injected for Low Back Pain and/or Pain Radiating Down the Leg

The prolotherapy injection sites are more numerous than trigger point therapy. But there is some overlap when it comes to myofascial pain, as this often overlays the trigger points.

In such cases, I will inject both the painful trigger zone in the deeper area and the fascial tissue through the same needle.

The structures marked out are the common areas that are injected in prolotherapy.

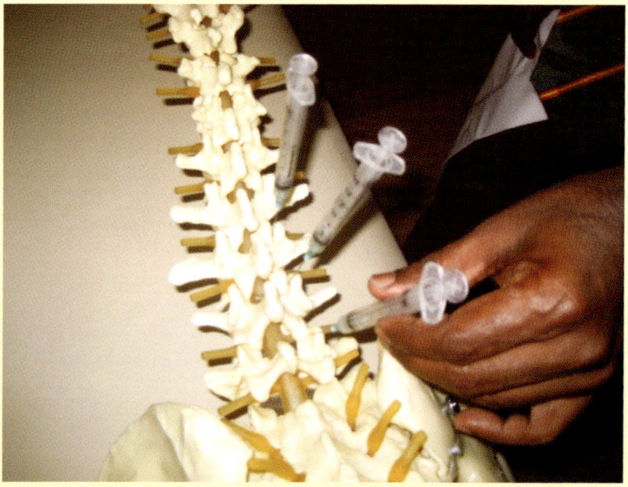

Photo 8.3: Prolotherapy Injection

This model indicates the deeper area where prolotherapy injections are administered. It is a procedure that is used when other methods have failed and the patient is likely to have back pain from weak ligaments and facet capsule.

The injections are not given into the spine, which many patients think. There is little complication from this procedure and significant pain relief can be expected.

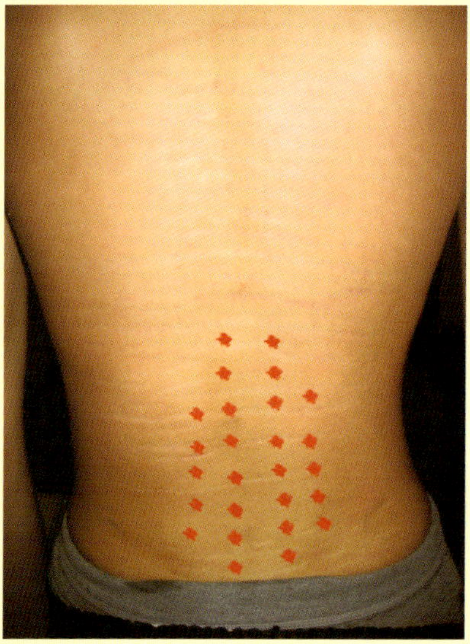

Photo 8.4: Injection Points

These are the common possible spots which are injected in trigger point therapy or prolotherapy.

1. Facet joints
2. Interspinous ligaments
3. Intertransverse ligaments
4. Myofascial covering of the muscles
5. Deep muscles of the spine

Prolotherapy

Prolotherapy involves the injection of a mildly irritant solution into an area of soft tissue injury and weakness, like the facet joint capsule or the low back ligaments. These tissues (called connective tissues) are weak and damaged. Injection into the area around the tissues stimulates an inflammatory response, and promotes healing (Photo 8.4). I have offered it to many of my patients in Johor and they provide good relief of pain.

The solution used is a local anaesthetic mixed with water, with/without a concentrated glucose (sugar) solution. If glucose cannot be used (e.g. with a diabetic patient), I use saline (salt) solution. Sarapin or glucosamine can also be used, if available. Many points (up to ten or more) may require injection, since it has to be done directly into the injured joint capsule and tendon areas. Injections can be repeated every three to six weeks till patient is pain-free.

Prolotherapy of the facet joints and sacroiliac joints of the low back has healed many of my patients who have had back pain for years. For many, the pain disappears immediately, due to the local anaesthetic effect. This tells me that the correct area has been injected. The pain may return for a day as the anaesthetic wears off. But as the inflammatory effect of healing starts, the pain starts to lessen after two or three days.

A recent European multicentre study shows significant improvement (of selected patients with back pain and/or leg pain) with use of O2/O3 (oxygen/ozone) and local anaesthetic injections into the paraspinal area (around the facet joints). The mechanism of action is probably by increasing the hydration (water content) in the area, and by reducing the molecules that irritate the nerve root and generate a pain reaction.

The difference between Prolotherapy Injections and Trigger Point Injections is that:

a. they treat different structures — ligaments and connective tissues in prolotherapy and painful muscle trigger points in trigger point injection; and

b. the injection solutions used are different — one intends to increase inflammation (prolotherapy) while the other reduces inflammation (trigger points).

Other Injection Treatments

Epidural Injection

This method has been used for many years. For those who have not responded to usual treatment or may have nerve pain down the leg, it has given good pain relief that can last for up to two years. The disadvantage is that it requires admission to hospital as it is usually done by an anaesthetist. A small volume of local anaesthetic and steroid is injected into the space between the bone and the spinal cord. This is a safe procedure and similar to an epidural injection given to pregnant women during labour (Photo 8.5).

I recommend this treatment after all the simple methods have been tried, and there is no indication on the X-rays that the patient needs surgery. Epidural is less often used because most patients with chronic pain seem to recover with trigger point injections and/or physiotherapy.

Nerve Root Sleeve Injection (NRSI)

This is similar to an epidural injection but more specifically placed in the nerve root sleeve, and not in the spinal epidural space. It can be used for back pain with nerve pain down the leg. The procedure requires the use of an X-ray image intensifier machine. The results are similar to epidural injection but the procedure is more difficult since the nerve root sleeve is harder to access. I do not recommend this procedure because the same results can be obtained by an epidural injection, which is simpler and cheaper.

Spinal Cord Electrical Stimulation

An electrical lead or leads are placed in the epidural space. The leads are connected to a battery which is placed under the skin in the buttock area (Diagram 8.6). Using an external remote control device, the patient can control the electrical impulses to the nerves, relieving the back pain. This technique probably works by interfering with the pain signals that go to the brain. It is only done when all other methods have not been successful in relieving pain. I do not recommend it because the pain relieving effects seem to be inconsistent.

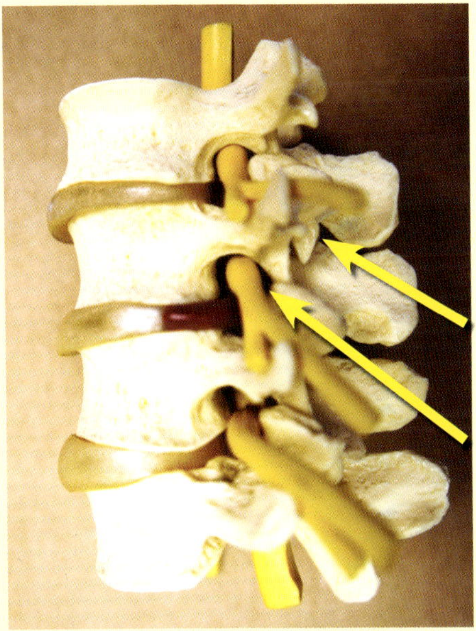

EPI — the needle is inserted centrally and a small volume of local anaesthetic and steroid is injected.

NRSI — the needle is placed closer to the nerve involved but requires X-ray control.

Photo 8.5: Epidural Injection

Epidural injection (EI) is a useful treatment when other methods have failed, especially when there is leg pain suggesting nerve root irritation. The top arrow shows the usual epidural that can be done as a one-day procedure by an anaesthetist. No other equipment is needed.

A more specific nerve root sleeve injection (NRSI) can be done, but is more difficult since it requires precise placement of the needle under X-ray control. It is done by interventional radiologists. NRSI seems to be more specific than EI, but the results are similar.

Given the ease and simplicity of the epidural procedure, I usually advise EI over the NRSI.

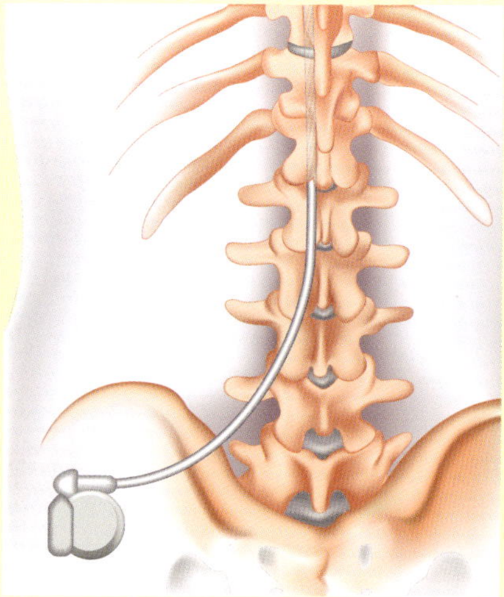

Diagram 8.6: Spinal Cord Stimulator

This procedure is used when there is severe, chronic pain not reduced by the other non-surgical methods or when there is intractable pain even after surgery for a definite structural cause.

The electrodes are introduced into the spinal space through an epidural procedure. The wires are connected to a battery that is inserted under the skin in the buttock (under local anaesthetic).

The current can be controlled using an external remote, and the patient is trained to use the device whenever the pain is severe.

9

Surgery for Low Back Problems

Surgery is done only for certain conditions and based on specific criteria. A small group of patients may need surgery early in their illness. In general, only one or two percent of patients may need surgery. Not all disc prolapses are an emergency.

> A 32-year-old patient saw me for back pain, with pain going down her right leg with some numbness. She had been treated by a doctor and went to a alternate medicine "sinseh" for many months. She requested an MRI scan which showed a slipped disc. She was afraid that she would be paralysed.
>
> I told her that she had to try medication, physiotherapy and back exercises. If she did not improve after some weeks, I would consider surgery. But if she did improve, we could wait and monitor her progress.

Many patients fear being paralysed. The chance of complete lower limb paralysis from a slipped disc or back pain is very rare. Just feeling some numbness of the outer side of the leg or mild weakness of the toe is not paralysis.

Before you read about the types of surgery available, it will be helpful to go back and read the causes of back pain. The type of surgery depends on what *structure* is believed to be the cause of the back pain.

Surgical Treatments

Discectomy (also called Fenestration and Discectomy)

Discectomy is done to remove the part of the prolapsed intervertebral disc that is pressing on a nerve. It is the commonest surgery done for a slipped disc. It can be done open (through a small incision) or as a microdiscectomy (using an even smaller incision and working through a microscope). Only the protruding disc material is removed, and the patient can get up and walk after one day. Patients are advised to resume normal activities as soon as they are pain-free. They need to strengthen the back muscles, and possibly take some anti-inflammatory medicine and nerve vitamins.

About two percent or less of patients with disc problems may need this operation (Diagram 9.1 and Photo 9.2).

Other Minimally Invasive Disc Removal Procedures

A number of pin-hole methods of disc removal/treatment are available. The common factor among all these methods is that a large needle or tube is inserted into the spinal disc under X-ray control. Through the tube or needle, various means can be used to remove or dissolve the damaged disc material. This includes mechanical burrs, ultrasound, laser, cryotherapy (cold freeze) and enzyme dissolution (Photo 9.3).

Laminectomy

The laminectomy operation involves the removal of the posterior bone covering the spinal cord. A laminectomy is done to get a better view and access to the spinal canal. Surgeons can then remove large free fragments of disc material and any growth or tumours. Patients with spinal stenosis have a very narrow spinal canal that compresses the spinal cord and nerves. Laminectomy increases the space available for the spinal cord and nerves (Diagram 9.4).

Spinal Fusion

Spinal fusion is an operation that joins two or more vertebral bones into one solid piece. It is usually done if there are abnormal movements

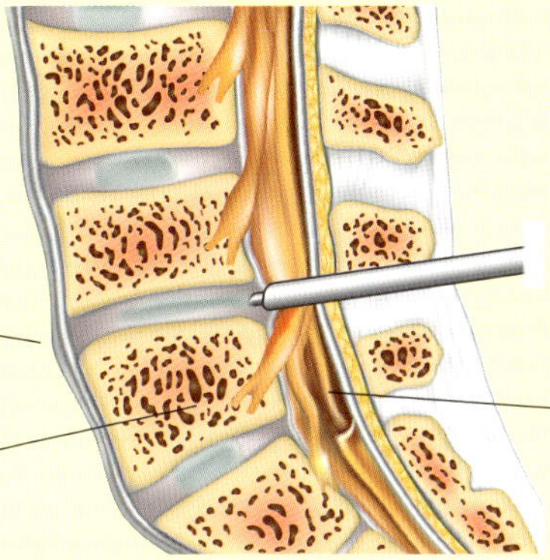

Diagram 9.1: Discectomy (Disc Removal)

The basic principle of this operation is to remove the disc material that has extruded into the spinal canal, causing nerve root compression.

This diagram shows a surgical instrument being inserted to remove the disc material that is pressing on the nerve. This instrument can be inserted through a larger incision (discectomy) or through the use of a microscope or video cameras (see text).

Whichever way the disc is removed, the leg pain is instantly healed. The patient is advised that the affected disc is now damaged and he should take preventive measures to prevent a recurrence of back pain.

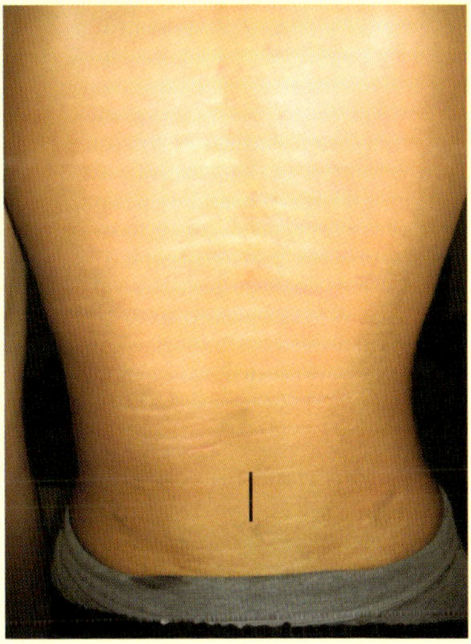

Photo 9.2: Discectomy

Operation is done through a small incision in the middle of the lower back (as marked).

This is the standard size incision I use for discectomy. Most patients are allowed to get up the next day and can go home after two days.

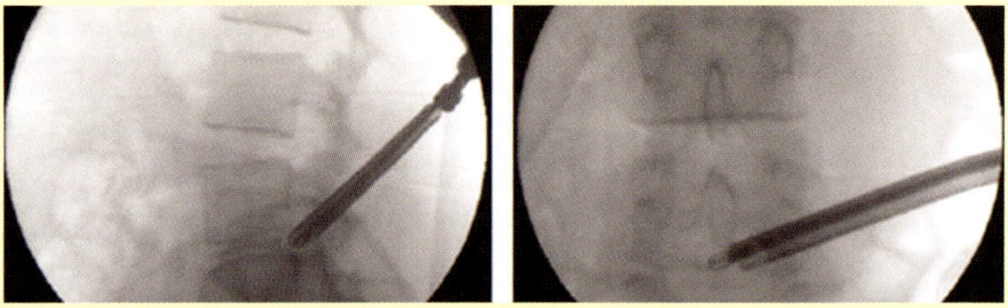

Photo 9.3: Discectomy Using a Microscope (Microdiscectomy)
This is an example of the use of a video camera and small puncture incisions to remove the disc material. The procedure is useful for selected indications, and a careful selection of patients is needed to avoid having to repeat the operation through a standard discectomy.

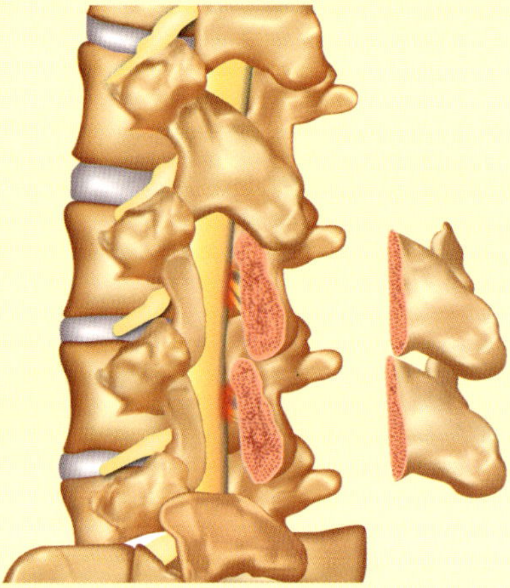

Diagram 9.4: Laminectomy
The laminectomy operation involves the removal of the spinous process and the bone overlying the spinal cord (the lamina). The diagram shows how much bone is removed and how the nerves of the spinal canal now have much more space.

The disadvantage of the procedure is that it involves the loss of some of the ligaments that support the spine and weakens some of the muscles. It is important to practise back prevention therapy and strengthen the back muscles without fail.

If doctors feel that the weakness may result in instability and pain, then the laminectomy is combined with a spinal fusion. This makes that bone segment one solid block.

between the bones or if bones are grinding on each other (osteoarthritis). Spinal fusion is usually done using bone taken from the pelvis or from a commercial bone bank. Some surgeons use metal screws and plates to hold the bones together.

A group of patients may continue to have some pain after spinal fusion, so it is important to also treat muscle, ligament and nerve causes of back pain. It is advisable to try all the other methods of treatment, including trigger point injections and prolotherapy, before considering spinal fusion (Diagram 9.5 and Photo 9.6).

Dynamic Lumbar Stabilisation

Unlike spinal fusion which solidly joins the two vertebral segments, this procedure limits the movement without completely stiffening the spine. The procedure is done from the back, and an implant can be placed between the spines of the vertebra. For added stability, screws and wires can be used. This procedure requires the use of X-ray controls, especially for the insertion of the screws. It is used on younger patients who have a degenerated disc causing back pain or nerve root compression (Diagram 9.7).

Artificial Disc Replacement

Another option for a worn-out disc that is causing pain or nerve compression is to insert an artificial disc to take the place of the worn-out disc. This procedure is done from the front (through the abdomen) and requires strict adherence to the criteria for the selection of patients (Photo 9.8).

Inter Spinous Process Decompression

This is a procedure that is used for single level spinal stenosis. In patients who have a single level disc degeneration, the vertebra are closer together. This reduces the spinal foramen space (the canal through which the nerve leaves the spine). A stiff metal spacer is placed between the spinous process (the bony projections at the back to the spine) corresponding

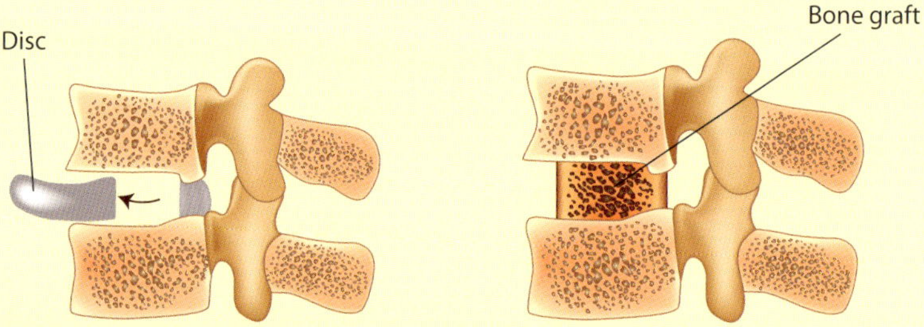

Examples of the use of metal implants are shown below:

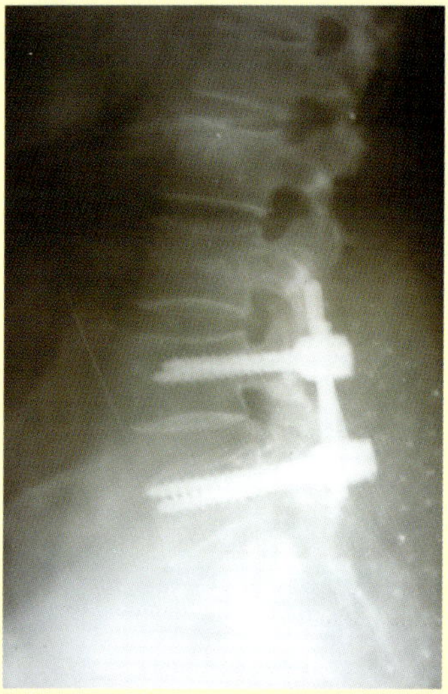

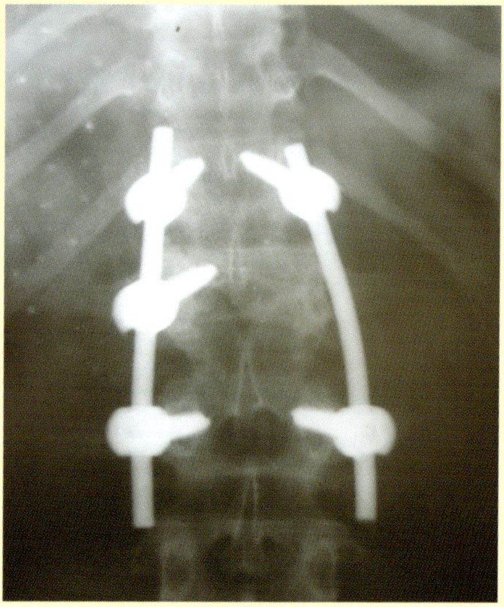

Diagram 9.5 and Photo 9.6: Lumbar Spinal Fusion

Spinal fusion essentially renders the intervertebral disc immobile. It can do this by (a) the removal of the disc material and inserting a bone graft taken from the pelvic area (see above) or (b) a bone graft can be inserted to the back of the spine to fuse the same segment.

The anterior or posterior approaches have the same result. The surgeon may choose either one depending on what the diagnosis is, and whether any other procedure is needed. For example, if a nerve needs to be decompressed, then the posterior route is more commonly done.

Many surgeons insert metal implants at the same time. The role of the implants is to secure immobility at the segment, allowing the bone graft to join into a strong union.

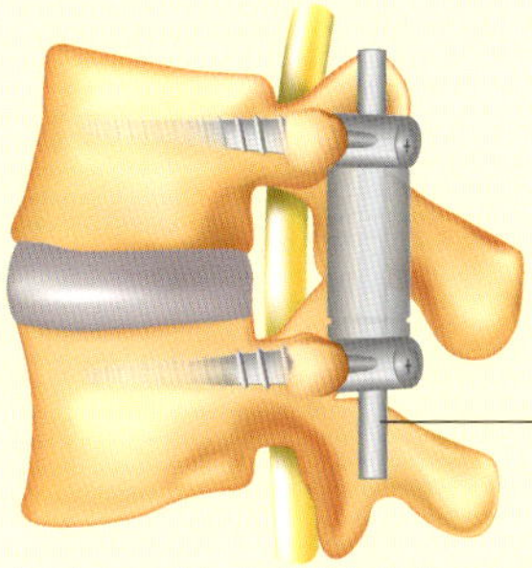

Diagram 9.7: Dynamic Lumbar Stabilisation

The principle of surgery in cases of degenerated disc with nerve root compression is that the nerve is mainly compressed when the body is bent backwards. Forward bending brings pain relief.

The implant reduces the extension of the spine but allows forward flexion. This flexibility is better than a full spinal fusion operation which stops all movement.

Together with the other preventive measures and back strengthening exercises, this procedure can help relieve pain in single-level problems.

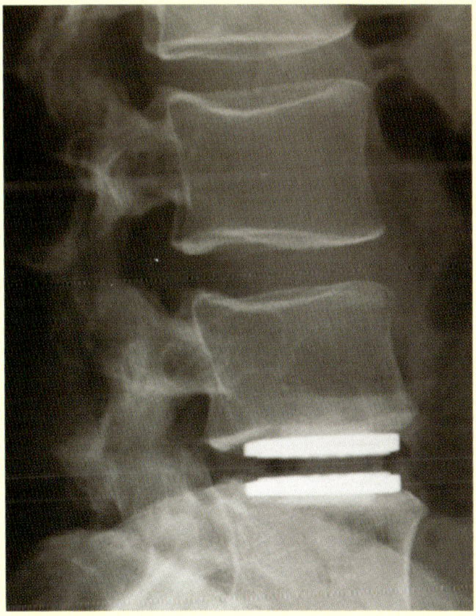

Photo 9.8: Artificial Disc Replacement

This is one of the different types of implants used today.

Disc replacement is becoming more common, as the benefits of maintaining some flexibility in the spine has been recognised. The implant technology has also advanced to a point where the implants are safe and give good results.

It is usually done for one or two level problems, usually associated with degenerative disc disease. The indications for disc replacement are very specific, so not all patients will need or benefit from this procedure. Generally, most patients will do well with a simple discectomy.

to the degenerated disc. If the patient has leg pain caused by nerve compression which is relieved by bending forward, this procedure can dramatically relieve the symptoms.

It is helpful for older patients who may not be suitable for general anaesthesia. The advantage is that the procedure can be done under a local anesthetic and the patient only needs a day in hospital (Diagram 9.9).

Spinal Curvature Correction

Corrective surgery can be done for a bent spine (scoliosis) to prevent complications later in life, especially back pain. A mildly bent spine is best left alone. More severely bent spines in the lower back can result in the "wear and tear" of the lower spine and may need correction (Photos 9.10 and 9.11).

This surgery requires the use of metal wires, rods and metal screws, and includes spinal fusion. Surgeons may use different methods but the aim is to straighten the spine. Many patients are in their late teens or early twenties. I operated on a patient with a severely bent spine twenty years ago. She remains pain-free, and is still able to work as a laundry worker.

Vertebroplasty and/or Kyphoplasty

This procedure is useful mainly for compression fractures of the lumbar vertebra caused by osteoporosis, where bone loss weakens and compresses the bone. A fresh compression fracture can be very painful and significantly disable an elderly person.

Under a local anaesthetic, a tube (like a drinking straw) is inserted into the fractured vertebra under X-ray control. An inflatable balloon is inserted and opens up the compressed vertebra. The cavity in the bone is filled with bone cement. This cement is similar to the dental cement used for filling teeth. It provides an immediate stability and internal fixation of the vertebra (Photo 9.12).

The procedure almost immediately relieves the pain of an osteoporotic compression fracture. The patient is then treated for osteoporosis.

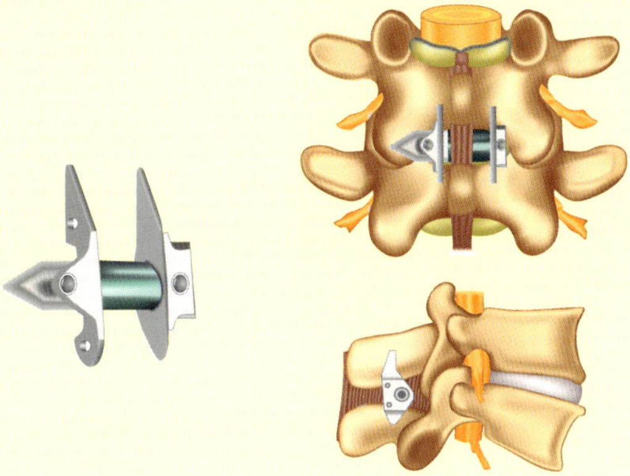

Diagram 9.9: Inter Spinous Process Decompression

Because of the simplicity of this procedure, which can be done in a day surgery centre, it can be used more frequently for one or two level degenerative disc disease with symptoms of spinal stenosis. This includes pain in the back and legs when walking or standing for long.

When the implant is inserted, it acts like an internal back splint. Combined with preventive measures and back strengthening exercises, it has been found to be very effective for a select group of patients.

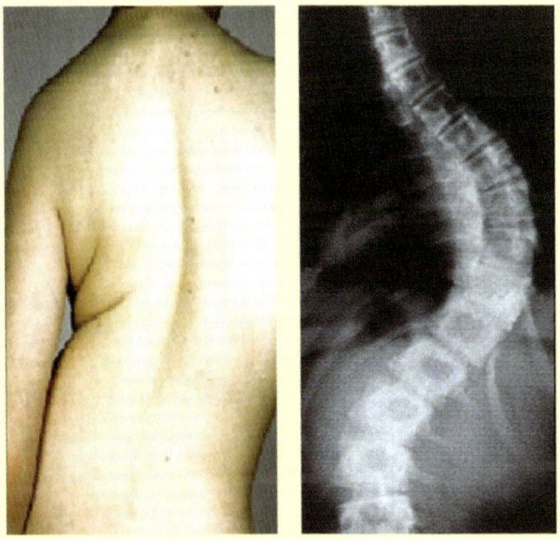

Photo 9.10: Scoliosis (Bent Spine)

Patients who have scoliosis generally do not complain of back pain till they are much older. The cause of back pain is usually traction (pulling) on the nerves or degeneration of the intervertebral discs and facet joints.

Patients who have severe curves are operated on for both cosmetic reasons and to prevent future problems. Some of these future complications are chest and heart problems, and back pain.

Many different implants are available and surgery can be done from the front of the spine or the back. In all cases, the correction is maintained by the implants while bone union is effected by the use of bone graft. The implants do not need to be removed in the future.

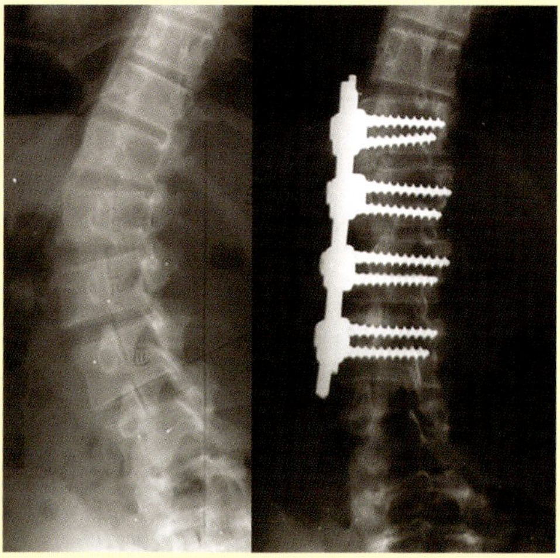

Photo 9.11: Scoliosis Correction

Once correction is done, X-rays are used to check if the curve remains in the corrected position. In this case, the correction is done from the front.

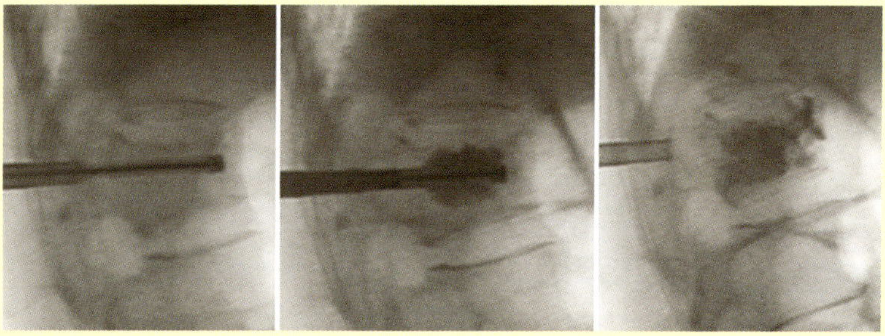

A compressed vertebral fracture causing pain.

Liquid bone cement is injected through a needle cannula.

The bone cement (black) hardens in the vertebra. Pain relief is immediate.

Photo 9.12: Vertebroplasy or Kyphoplasty Using Bone Cement

This procedure involves injecting bone cement into the compressed fracture of the vertebral body. As the cement hardens, it stabilises the fracture like an internal splint, providing almost immediate pain relief to the patient.

For older patients with osteoporosis, this procedure affords very good results. It is done in a hospital under X-ray control. The patient usually stays overnight before going home.

Final Thoughts on Surgery for Low Back Pain

Each method is useful for certain selected patients. Your surgeon will have to carefully explain to you which methods are most suitable, based on your complaints and signs, as well as the MRI and other findings. You can then make an informed decision.

Do not be misled into thinking that if you have a prolapsed "slipped" disc, all the methods have the same results. Each patient is different. The vast majority of patients can recover without surgery. With the success of non-surgical special treatments for chronic back pain (e.g. trigger point inactivation or prolotherapy), it is possible for most patients to avoid surgery.

Section III

The Prevention of Low Back Pain

10

Protection of the Low Back

"It is always wise to protect the back, whether you have back pain or not"

Most of the back pain caused by injuries and damage to the bone or cartilage can recover quite well over time. Unfortunately, some patients develop chronic back pain that comes and goes for months and years. It is difficult in these circumstances to know which structure of the spine is causing the pain. That is why prevention is better than cure.

How can you protect your back against chronic or recurrent low back pain?

There are many misconceptions and disagreements about what is good and what is bad. Below is a list of what has been proven useful through evidence-based studies:

Preventive Measures for Body Structure Problems

Back pain caused by bone or cartilage injury can heal, but leave weakened muscles and ligaments which contribute to persistent pain or pain that keeps coming back. Patients need to look after their posture and reduce the daily stresses on their lower back.

Muscle Strengthening

To prevent recurrence of backache, it is important to strengthen your back and abdomen muscles.

Strong back and abdominal muscles are important to help relieve back pain and prevent pain from recurring. My patients do not complain that it is hard to do. Unfortunately, *many forget to do the exercises when they are pain-free.* They remember only when the back pain comes back.

Many types of exercises are available. I recommend a simplified routine that strengthen mainly the back and the abdomen muscles. The exercises take less than 5 minutes a day. I highly recommend that even people who do not suffer from backache strengthen their backs (see Back Exercises Chart in Chapter 14).

Standing

If you have to stand a lot during the day or at work, make sure you learn a good posture.

The spine has three normal curves. Learning to stand properly will help prevent back and neck problems. If you do the muscle exercises regularly, your posture will improve. The pressure in the intervertebral discs of the spine is actually lower when you are standing than when you are sitting (Diagram 10.1).

Sitting

If you have to sit all day at work, it is important to sit in a comfortable position and to change positions regularly. But some general principles do apply (Diagram 10.2).

If you work in an office, make sure that your work chair is comfortable for you. There is no single best position for sitting. If you are spending hours on a chair, your chair should be able to tilt and change positions. Then, you can keep adjusting your chair based on how you feel through the day. Make sure your feet can be placed flat on the ground. A chair that is too high stresses the spine. You can use a small foot stool if necessary. Avoid bar stools and chairs where your legs have to hang down.

If you have a job which requires that you sit for hours, it is advisable to get up every half hour just to relax or stretch. Why not stand up to answer the phone or talk to a colleague?

Walking

If you have to walk all day at work or elsewhere, proper footwear is essential.

It is easy to neglect the importance of footwear, since it may seem to have no relationship with back pain. However, poor footwear can cause either foot pain, knee pain, back pain or all three. If you spend a lot of

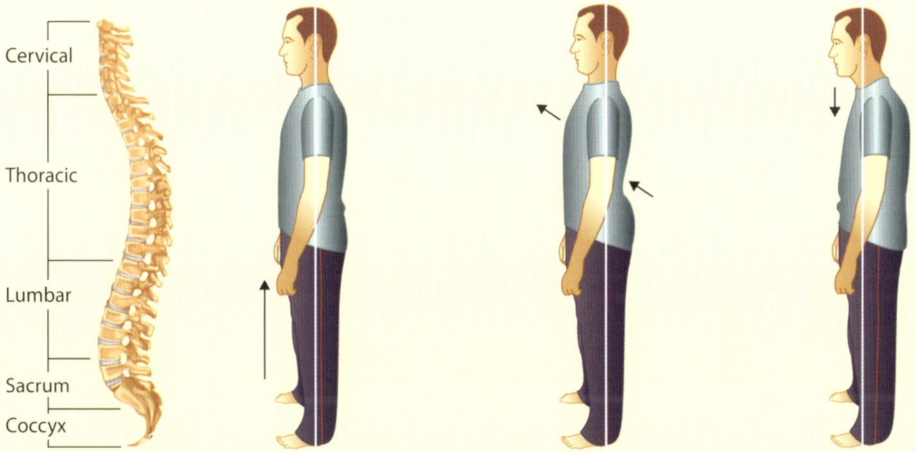

Curvatures of the spine:

Cervical — Neck
Thoracic — Upper Back
Lumbar — Lower Back

Correct Posture:

Maintains the normal curves of the spine and the body weight is transmitted through the centre of gravity.

Incorrect Posture:

Trying to have a straight back makes the body weight transmitted behind the centre of gravity. This strains the muscles and the facet joints.

Incorrect Posture:

Hunching forward seems comfortable these days, but it makes the body weight transmit in front of the centre of gravity. The back muscles and ligaments, and the discs, are subjected to increased workload, causing pain.

Diagram 10.1: Standing Posture

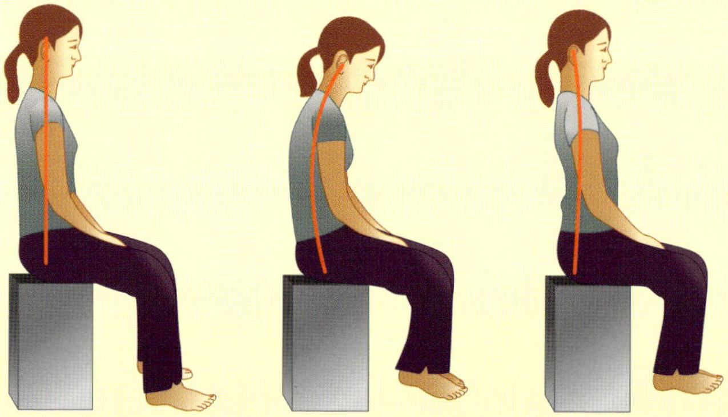

Better Posture:

The better posture maintains the normal curvature of the spine, so that the body weight is transmitted through the centre of gravity. Spend most of the time in this posture.

Incorrect Posture:

The body weight is too forward compared to the centre of gravity. The muscles of the back and ligaments are strained, causing pain. This position can be used for short periods only.

Incorrect Posture:

The body weight is transmitted behind the centre of gravity. The back muscles and ligaments are strained, causing pain. This position is used for short periods only to stretch the back.

Diagram 10.2: Sitting Posture

Diagram 10.3: High Heels Affect Posture

The body weight is transmitted in front of the centre of gravity, thus putting great strain on the muscles of the back and ligaments supporting the vertebra.

Another effect is pain in the forefoot due to increased pressure.

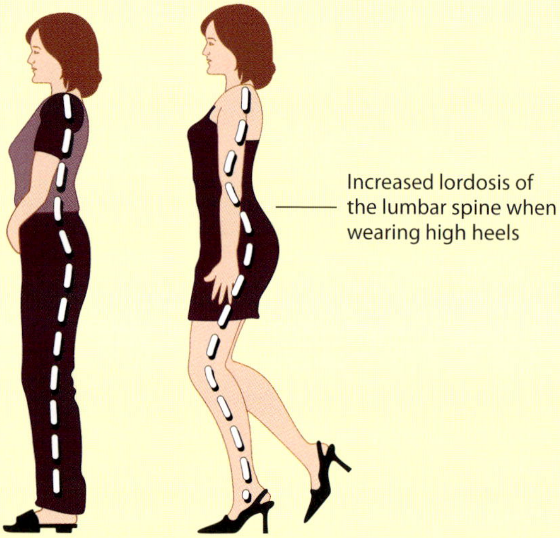

time walking or standing, your footwear, should be comfortable, fit your feet well, and give support when making sudden turns. A cushioned heel in the shoe softens the impact of each step on the spine.

High-heel Shoes: High heels increase the curvature (lordosis) of the lower spine. This puts abnormal stress on the muscles, ligaments and joints of the spine. High heels should be used for short periods only, e.g. at parties (Diagram 10.3).

Slippers: When going for long walks, avoid slippers or flip flops slippers. Slippers do not provide support for the ankle and foot, and makes the foot and toes work harder as you walk. This puts pressure on the spine (Diagram 10.4).

Strapless Shoes: Patients should also avoid shoes that are strapless, especially if they are walking a lot. The lower limb muscles have to work harder and this stresses the spine.

Arch Support: Foot imbalance (e.g. pronation/in-toeing) can stress the lower spine and hips. Use a good pair of walking shoes. If you use dress shoes to work, buy shoes with an arch support, or buy an arch support and insert it into your shoes (Diagram 10.5).

Orthotics: If the heel of your shoe is wearing out unevenly, you probably need orthotics to balance your foot. Orthotics balance the way you walk, and protect the back and knees during daily activities. Do note that custom-made orthotics are expensive (Diagram 10.6).

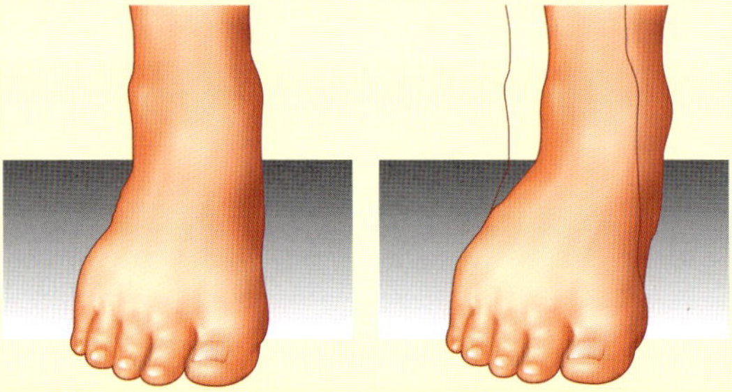

At the impact of the foot on the ground, the foot remains in a neutral position.

Without support, the foot tends to move inward (pronate) as it takes a full step. This is fine for short periods, but if someone walks for long periods or tries to run with slippers, the foot will be imbalanced, and can result in back pain and calf/foot problems.

Diagram 10.4: Position of Foot with Slippers (Flip Flops)

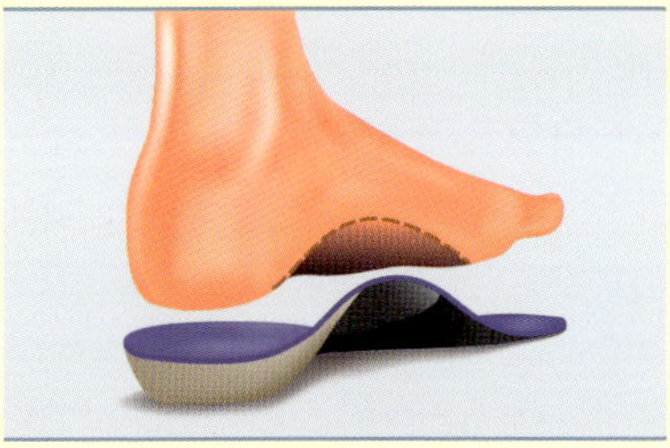

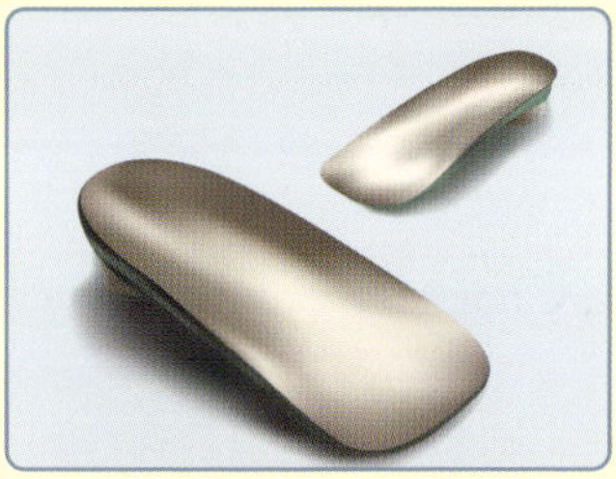

Diagram 10.5: Proper Shoes Provide Support

When walking for long periods, the arch support prevents the foot from pronating. This will, in the long run, protect against foot, calf, knee and back pain.

Diagram 10.6: Orthotic Shoe Inserts

Made of harder plastic than the normal cushion supports in shoes, these orthotics give better support for those whose feet may be imbalanced.

Check how the heel of your shoe is wearing out or visit an orthotist to see whether you need a hard orthotic insert.

When walking, well-balanced feet can protect against low back pain.

Be Flexible

Even if you are not an active person, you should do simple back stretching for five minutes a day. It will protect you from sudden back injuries/pain.

As people age, their joints become stiffer. This stiffness also affects the facet joints and the ligaments of the spine. Research shows that keeping the spine flexible reduces the chance of back pain coming back. Simple stretching exercises are recommended for everyone.

- Do stretching for two to five minutes every day.
- Just stretch till you feel a bit tight, then stop.

Sleeping Position

In general, the most comfortable position is the best position. If you are comfortable and are sleeping well, do not worry. If you sleep in a position that is causing pain, then you need to change. For low back protection, it is important to maintain the natural curve of the lower spine when you sleep.

- If you lie on your back, have a small pillow under your knees. This helps patients who have backache to sleep better (Diagram 6.1, Chapter 6).

- If you sleep on your side, keep your legs together and bend at the hip and knee. Put a pillow between the legs for comfort (Photo 6.2, Chapter 6).

Mattress

It is not necessary to sleep on a piece of wood or the floor. If you are still having back pain in the morning, change your mattress. There is no one "good" mattress. Keep trying different ones till you find one that is *comfortable*. You do not have to spend money on the expensive electric beds that are advertised.

External Pressure on the Nerve

A wallet in the back pocket can cause back pain. Men who carry their wallets in the back pocket have to sit on the wallet or adjust themselves when they are sitting. If you sit for long periods, this bad alignment makes the back muscles work harder. Some men complain of pain running down the leg. This is because the wallet is compressing the sciatic nerve onto the femur bone. More specifically, it can cause piriformis syndrome type pain. It can mimic a nerve compression pain from the spine (Diagram 10.7).

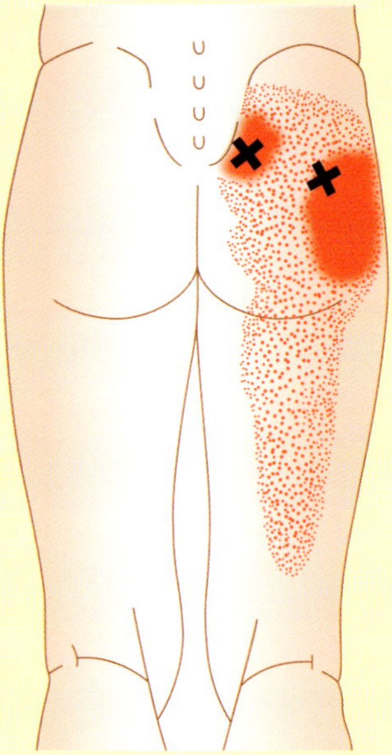

Diagram 10.7: Back Pocket Wallet Pain
Some patients who sit on their wallet can feel pain in the piriformis area (because of the pressure of the wallet that compresses the sciatic nerve on the femur at the level of the piriformis muscle.

Avoid carrying a large wallet in the back pocket.

Carrying Everyday Objects

A person can get back pain from carrying bags incorrectly, so the principle is to avoid tilting the spine when carrying a load.

School bags are heavy and cause a tilt in the spine. Students should carry school bags on the back, and not on one side. Even better, use a rolling bag. Women should make sure their handbags are not heavy. Otherwise, they will tilt to one side when they walk, thus straining the back.

Be careful when carrying heavy groceries. The temptation is to carry all the bags in one hand and use the other hand, for example, to open a door. *If you have a lot of groceries, carry equal weights in both hands.* Then, you will be stable. You can put the bags down to open the door or look for car keys.

Lifting Objects or Twisting the Back

Many people have muscle (and maybe "wear and tear") weakness in their back, particularly if they are older. Even if light loads are lifted incorrectly, pain can result.

The principle is to use the hips and knees when lifting objects. Get into the habit of bending your knees to pick things up from the ground. When driving a car, never twist to take things from the back seat. Always stop, get out and open the back door to take out your bag. Do not forget the rules of lifting when travelling. Always carry bags on both sides and ask for help when lifting heavy bags into the car or overhead bins in an airplane.

Maintaining Good Health

Patients who have suffered backache may have other health problems as well. The tissues in the spine need to be healthy to prevent problems. A balanced diet of proteins, carbohydrates and fat, with calcium, vitamins and minerals, helps keep tissues healthy.

Vitamin Supplements

Vitamin and mineral supplements can help the healing of damaged tissues and keep tissues healthy.

Weight lifters and body builders take vitamins and minerals to build up muscles. A simple and inexpensive multivitamin supplement is all that is needed. I recommend that patients take multivitamins, calcium and vitamin B (e.g. B12) regularly, even after the pain is gone. It can take tissues in the spine up to nine months to fully heal.

Body Weight

Obesity can contribute to back pain. Lower back muscles and structures are stressed by the extra weight.

If you are overweight, try to control your diet when recovering from a backache. This can be done by a balanced diet and avoiding fast foods. A daily exercise regime helps, as well as advice from a dietician.

Other Medical Conditions

Some diseases like diabetes or gout can affect tissue healing. They may also perpetuate inflammation in the joints or muscles. Intestinal problems like constipation can cause or contribute to back pain (viscerogenic back pain). Proper diet often reduces this problem.

Summary

In general, eat a healthy and balanced diet. Eat and drink in moderation. Take at least one to two litres of water every day. Take vitamins and mineral supplements. Go for a walk or exercise every other day. And do not forget exercises and stretching for your back.

Stress Reduction

A big predictor of recurrent back pain is actually a person's daily level of stress. Many medical studies confirm that it does play a part in persistent back pain.

When no other cause can be found for chronic back pain, patients should look at their daily stress as a possible cause. Unfortunately, patients do not like these kinds of questions, and tend to be defensive or even deny it without even thinking about it. Everyone has some stress at some time in their life, and stress can result in emotional or physical problems or both.

Why Does Stress Cause Physical Pain?

Stress causes real pain by causing increased muscle tension and inflammations in soft tissues through increased blood levels of corticoid hormones. Daily stress can cause headache, neck pain and gastric ulcer pain. In some patients, stress causes back pain.

- Are you stressed at work? How do you get along with other employees? Are you worried you may lose your job? Do you feel better when you are not at work?
- Any problems in your family? Have you lost a loved one? Any marital problems?
- Any financial problems?
- Are you anxious about dying? Do you wonder about life?

Seek spiritual peace or hobbies that can help you reduce stress. Where stress appears to be aggravating the backache, medication can help reduce stress. Stress-relieving medications (e.g. SSRIs) generally have lower side effects and can significantly reduce chronic back pain.

11

Osteoporosis — A Brief Overview

Osteoporosis is a serious women's health problem today, of which the first sign of osteoporosis is often back pain. It is a major cause of morbidity (ill health) and mortality. It is estimated that a woman who sustains an osteoporotic spinal fracture has a 10 to 15% higher mortality in the first year. She also faces five times the risk of developing new fractures (e.g. hip fractures) that require surgery. This increases the mortality rate even more.

Menopausal women or women over the age of 50 are recommended to go for osteoporosis screening. Many orthopaedic clinics now have simple ultrasound screening bone densitometers, while bigger hospitals may have the more accurate DEXA bone density machines.

What is Osteoporosis?

Osteoporosis is a condition resulting in the loss of bone mass. The bone structure becomes weaker, and can develop small cracks. In severe osteoporosis, the spinal bones can crumble and flatten. Many vertebra bones may flatten over the years, giving rise to pain or deformity (e.g. a hunch back).

It is important to recognise the possibility of osteoporosis as the cause of back pain, especially in women. Simple activities like twisting the back, sneezing, lifting a chair or opening a window may cause a crack or mild compression fractures.

Why Can it Cause Back Pain?

The cracks and/or fractures in the bone irritate the nerves nearby, thus causing pain (Photo 11.1).

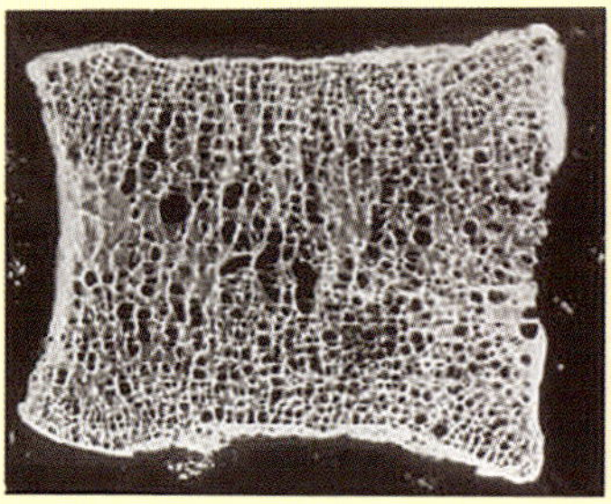

Normal Vertebra

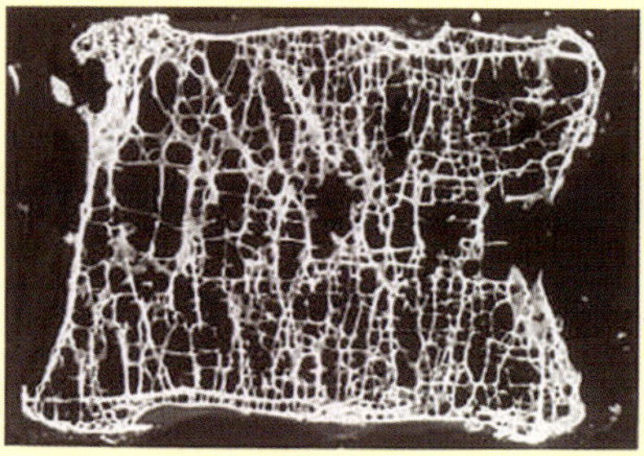

Osteoporotic Vertebra

Photo 11.1: Normal Bone and "Weak Bone" (Osteoporosis)

The left image shows a normal bone. The bone consists of bony trabecula that fill up the body of the vertebra. Osteoporosis is not the softening of bone but the loss of bone — the loss of bony trabecula to be precise. The vertebra on the right is osteoporotic, and the thin and brittle trabecula are very obvious. It is no surprise that fractures can happen with minimal trauma, like opening a window or bending over.

Treatment consists of maintaining and supporting the bone that is left and stimulating new bone formation. Various medications are prescribed based on these considerations, depending on the degree of osteoporosis. Backache caused by osteoporotic fractures are hard to treat by medication alone, so it is very important for all women to take precautions. Various risk factors are described in the text.

What Causes Osteoporosis?

Generally, bone loss occurs with age. But after menopause, women lose bone mass faster than men because of the loss of female hormones (estrogen).

What Factors Result in a Woman Getting Osteoporosis?

Higher risk of osteoporosis is found in women:

- of Chinese or Caucasian ancestry
- who are thin or underweight
- who do not do much exercise, smoke cigarettes, drink excessive alcohol, have a high caffeine intake and /or with a low dietary calcium intake
- who have early menopause, and/or
- have a family history of osteoporosis.

How Can Osteoporosis be Prevented and Treated?

Bone loss can be slowed by having a good intake of calcium and vitamin D every day. The usual medications to treat osteoporosis are calcitonin, bisphosphanates or hormone treatment.

All osteoporosis patients (especially those who have had a fracture) are recommended to take bisphosphanates and calcium. If they have back pain, calcitonin is given till the pain is reduced. Bisphosphanates strengthens bones and reduces the occurrence of fracture, and can be given as a weekly or monthly pill, or by a once-yearly injection.

What Can Young Women Do to Prevent Osteoporosis in Old Age?

Young women should reduce the risk factors within their control. They should take adequate calcium and vitamin D from their teenage years. They should not smoke, and they should minimise alcohol and coffee intake. Women should exercise (e.g. walk or jog) regularly since it helps strengthen the bones.

Women should have a bone density measurement when they reach menopause and every two years thereafter. A simple bone density screening is done in some clinics and hospitals. If diagnosed, osteoporosis therapy is a lifelong treatment.

Section IV

Understanding Issues in Low Back Pain

12

Common Patient Mistakes

1. Waiting Too Long

Do not wait too long to see a doctor. If you have back pain for over three weeks, it is better to have it examined.

2. Not Patient with Treatment

Do not rush from doctor to doctor or try all kinds of alternate treatment without giving the treatments time to work. Most doctors work step by step to help patients. Back problems take time to heal.

3. Resting Too Long

It is now known that too much bed rest or not moving much is actually bad for the back. Once you feel a bit better, get up and walk around, and try to be active. Start and continue back exercises and stretching as soon as possible.

4. Taking Too Much Medicine

Painkillers are useful for a short time. If you need painkillers for over a week, you should see a specialist.

5. Persisting with Unproven Treatments

Since back pain is common and difficult to treat, many people feel helpless about their chronic pain. In this atmosphere of pain and uncertainty, it is easy to believe the recommendations of friends or advertised treatments or devices for back pain. There is a difference between anecdotal evidence and evidence-based medicine. Always ask the tough questions to anyone (even doctors) who recommends a type of treatment to you.

6. Rushing into Surgery

I have noticed that patients are often excessively worried about possible paralysis. Some patients go for surgery much too soon, before trying physiotherapy or injection treatments. Always ask for the alternatives to surgery before you make a decision.

7. Neglecting Preventive Measures

Preventive measures are recommended for one reason — they work! The main reason why many patients come back to see me is that they forgot to follow the advice given for the long-term care of their back.

13

Case Studies of Back Pain Patients

How most patients come to the clinic and the usual methods of treatment

You may be reading this book chapter by chapter. However, if you are not in the medical field, it might be difficult to understand how it applies in real life.

One way to put all the information in this book together is to give you examples of how patients may come to see me for back pain. You can then refer to the relevant chapters to be able understand how the cause of back pain is diagnosed and why certain test and treatment are done.

I will describe the common causes of the symptoms, and give the common recommended treatments. However, no two patients are the same. There will be variations in treatment, but the general principles will be followed.

Acute Back Pain Scenarios *(e.g. sudden pain of less than two weeks in duration)*

Case 1: Severe back pain for one day

A 30-year-old lady felt a sudden backache when she bent and lifted her baby at 8am. She came to the clinic at 5pm, slightly bent over and she could not walk straight because the pain was getting worse. There was no pain or numbness in the legs.

The pain is usually in the low back (middle or side). From her history, the cause is probably a muscle pull (resulting in a cramp) or a possible muscle injury (tear). The pain gets worse over the next few hours because the injured or cramped muscle does not relax, causing inflammation in the surrounding areas.

The usual treatment is a painkilling medicine or injection, ice pack to the low back, anti-inflammatory medication (NSAID) and muscle relaxant tablets for a few days.

After childbirth, her tissues may still be weak due to the hormonal changes of pregnancy. She should be advised on good nourishment, vitamin supplements and the protection of her back. She must start back exercises once the pain is better. This is because the period of rest after injury weakens the back muscles. She should continue the exercises to strengthen her back.

Almost all patients with this type of sudden injury will recover without problem. Many do not come for a follow up. If she has mild residual chronic pain, she may benefit from physiotherapy (deep heat like ultrasound) to the painful area.

Case 2: Severe back pain for three days, much worse on the 3rd day

A 30-year-old man felt a sudden backache when he lifted a heavy box onto his lorry three days ago. The pain did not bother him much but got worse the next day. The third day, he could not sleep and was unable to work. He had no leg pain or numbness.

The pain and tenderness are usually in the middle or sides of the low back. The causes can be a spinous ligament injury, a tear of the back muscle or an injury to the intervertebral disc. Because we cannot be sure if he has any pre-existing bone problem, an X-ray is helpful.

The initial treatment is the same as Case #1. This type of injury, being more severe, may take longer to heal. The treatment will thus be continued till his symptoms subside.

Special note: If the X-ray shows a defect in the bone (e.g. spondylolysis/listhesis) or possible cartilage problem (e.g. decreased intervertebral sic space), then he will be asked to come back in a week for another examination. A re-examination when the pain is less helps rule out other problems.

This patient may take two weeks or more to fully recover. Most patients will recover fully by six weeks. It is important to allow this amount of time for healing. Medications can be given during this time, including muscle relaxants, anti-inflammatories and vitamins. He can get up and ambulate when he feels better, but may need to avoid work for a few weeks. He should start back exercises when the pain is less. If recovery is slow, physiotherapy will help. He will also be told about how to protect his back, and take the necessary precautions when lifting loads.

Case 3: Severe back pain for three days, much worse on the 3rd day, with right leg pain and numbness

A 30-year-old man felt a sudden backache when he lifted a heavy box onto his lorry three days ago. The pain did not bother him much but got worse the next day. The third day, he could not sleep and was unable to work. He had right leg pain and numbness along the outer side of the leg up to his toes.

The pain is in the middle of the low back and right buttock area. The cause, based on his story, is either an injury of the spine and/or buttock muscles, or injury to the intervertebral disc (with possible disc protrusion). Because we cannot be sure of prior problems, an X-ray is helpful. We will also ensure that he has not got paralysis of both lower limbs, and/or problems passing urine or bowel motions.

The initial treatment is the same as Cases #1 and #2. This is despite the fact that he feels some pain in his leg. In most cases, the nerve root is not compressed but just irritated, so we can treat him the same way as someone who has only back pain and not the other symptoms.

The patient should rest in a position he feels comfortable and given painkillers, muscle relaxants and vitamin B6 and B12. He may also need sleeping tablets and anti-inflammatory medicines. He should be checked again and given a follow-up appointment.

After a few days to a week, there should be evidence of recovery. The regular treatment is then continued and he can walk around and ambulate around his home. He should not return to heavy work for a few weeks.

If there is no evidence of recovery, if the pain is getting worse or if the right leg pain and numbness are more severe, then an MRI scan is needed to establish any structural cause for the pain.

In general, the majority of patients who come with this combination of symptoms will significantly improve by six weeks, and can resume heavy work after three months. Those who do not recover, even after special non-surgical treatments and/or injections, and have a prolapsed disc confirmed on an MRI scan, will need surgery.

Case 4: Severe backache for three days after a fall from a tree

A 30-year-old man falls from a rambutan tree and has severe low back pain. He has been resting at home, and had some herbs and local medicines applied to his back. He has been unable to sleep. He has no leg pain or weakness. He is unable to sit or stand, and has severe pain in the area around the centre of the lower spine when he moves in bed.

Here the fall and severe localised pain suggest a bone injury. The most likely cause is a fracture. For all patients with a history of a fall or major accident, with severe pain and difficulty in turning, sitting or walking, an X-ray must be done. An X-ray would usually reveal a stable compression fracture of the vertebra. In the even rarer event that there is no fracture seen on X-ray, an MRI scan will be needed to make sure that the patient does not have a hidden fracture or has an injury to the intervertebral disc or ligaments of the spine.

For a simple and stable fracture, initial treatment is again like Case #3.

Stronger injection painkillers are needed. The patient may need to be admitted to hospital where there are nurses to help him for toilet purposes. Once the pain subsides (usually in about two or three weeks), he is allowed to stand or walk, using a back brace or lumbar support. If patient asks to go home, he has to use the back brace to protect the spine for at least six weeks. Generally, stable fractures of the spine heal well and do not need surgery unless there are nerve compression problems or symptoms of paralysis, and/or difficulty passing urine and bowel motions.

It takes at least 12 weeks for the fracture to heal fully. A heavy manual worker is usually advised to be off work for three to six months. If the patient strengthens his back muscles and does flexibility exercises, he can protect his back from chronic pain in future.

Case 5: Severe backache for three days after a fall from a tree

Exactly as in case 4, but the X-ray shows an unstable fracture.

If the injury was very severe, the fracture will be unstable. Unstable fractures have the potential to move out of place if the patient gets up and walks too early or if he is moved without protection. Movement in the spine may cause nerve damage. In this situation, admission to hospital is needed.

The regular and long term treatment is like Case #4.

The patient will need to spend three to six weeks in the hospital bed, with regular turning, till the bone becomes strong enough to allow him to get up. In rare cases, depending on the type of fracture, surgery is needed to make the spine stable. This is done by holding the bones together with some metal screws or wire and doing a spinal fusion.

Long-term exercises help reduce future back problems. However, most patients are advised not to return to any heavy lifting or heavy work.

Chronic Back Pain (Low Back Pain That Lasts For Weeks And Months)

Case 6: Low back pain for last six months, occasionally very painful

A 45-year-old lady, who had severe back pain one year ago, has been feeling back pain off and on for the last six months. Once in a while, the pain can be severe but lessens after a few days. Her life is affected because she cannot do housework, and cannot sit or stand for long periods at a time.

When tested by direct pressure, she had pain in both buttocks and the lower spine. Otherwise, everything is normal. X-rays are taken and show no bone problem. Her symptoms do not require an MRI scan.

The chronic back pain in this lady is mostly due to muscle and soft tissue problems. She has tender trigger points where the muscle is in isolated spasm and inflammation. There is also tenderness of the ligaments of the spine. She has weakness of the back muscles. It is noted that she stopped all back exercises and preventive measures about three months after she recovered from her first attack of back pain.

Treatment will begin by starting her on back exercises and preventive measures. Together with these general measures, we will have to inactivate the trigger zones in the buttocks and lower spine. Trigger point treatment using physiotherapy, massage, acupuncture, ultrasound or manual therapy can take two to four weeks before the patient shows improvement.

If patient has already seen many doctors, taken many medicines and/or done physiotherapy or seen traditional medicine practitioners without success, then direct injection of the trigger spots and/or prolotherapy is an effective step. Patients usually feel better after one or two days, and can be pain-free within a week.

Once pain-free, patient must continue back exercises and back stretching to maintain flexibility. These preventive measures reduce the recurrence of low back pain.

Case 7: Low back pain for the last six months, occasionally very painful. Had prolapsed disc two years ago

A 45-year-old lady who had severe backache and right leg pain (diagnosed as "prolapsed intervertebral disc") two years ago, recovered after three months of non-surgical treatment. But after 15 months of no pain, she has been feeling back pain off and on for the last six months. Once in a while, the pain can be severe, but gets better after a few days. Her life is affected because she cannot do housework. When the back pain comes, she also feels pain in the right leg and some numbness of the lower leg.

This patient recovered well from a prolapsed ("slipped") disc, but now gets occasionally severe back pain with leg pain. The X-ray in this patient will probably show a narrowed intervertebral disc with "wear and tear" changes (osteoarthritis). She will have pain on trigger points in the right buttock and the right side of the back along the facet joints.

This recurrence of pain arises from more than one structure — muscle tightness due to weak back muscles, soft tissue weakness due to wear and tear at the facet joints, and "wear and tear" of the intervertebral disc, causing decreased movements and irritation of the adjacent nerve root. It is known that an injured intervertebral disc can progress to disc degeneration over time or as the patient gets older.

The general treatment plan is the same as Case #6.

It may take some weeks for the patient to feel better, and if non-surgical methods do not work, injection therapy or prolotherapy can give good relief. This patient may also be given vitamins, calcium and glucosamine supplements.

Muscle strengthening and flexibility exercises, and preventive measures are instituted to reduce the recurrence of back and leg pain.

In the event that leg pain is severe and is the predominant symptom, and if there is little relief with non-surgical treatments, then a repeat MRI scan may be needed to check whether there is spinal fusion and/or any significant nerve root compression that may require surgery.

Case 8: Mild back pain for the last six months, occasionally very painful

A 55-year-old lady had back pain after she twisted her back lifting a pail of water. She initially had severe pain which lessened after a few weeks. But recently, she has continuous, moderate pain in her low back. She is unable to do much housework or walk long distances. The pain lessens when she lies down. She had early menopause at age 45, has been smoking since age 20 and does not drink milk (she takes black coffee).

On examination, she has a small but obvious bone "lump" in the centre of the lower back. The lump is tender (painful on direct pressure). When she stands, it is noted that she is hunching forward. The X-ray in this patient is likely to show osteoporosis of the bone and a collapse fracture of one (or more) of the lumbar vertebra.

In osteoporosis, the pain mainly comes from the osteoporotic fractures within the vertebra (which can range from small cracks to a full collapse of the vertebra when she twists her back). There will also be pain arising from the weak surrounding muscles and weakness of the spinal ligaments. Direct pressure on the low back muscles will also reveal painful trigger zones, which are a response to the bone/muscle/ligament weakness. In osteoporosis, trigger zones can also be present all along the lower spine ligaments and buttocks.

The general treatment plan is the same as Case #1.

It will take about three to six weeks for the fracture pain to lessen. A lumbar support may help for a few days if the pain is severe. She should ambulate around the house within the limits of her pain.

In the long term, she must do a bone density measurement and be treated for osteoporosis. This includes a bone strengthening medicine (e.g. bisphosphanates), calcium and Vitamin D supplements. If osteoporosis is severe, she may need calcitonin (the injection or nasal calcitonin may help reduce the pain).

She must understand that she will have to be on osteoporosis medications, and preventive therapy for years to come. She must look after herself to avoid repeat injury. Many patients stop the osteoporosis treatment when they feel better but this guarantees that the pain will come back after a few months. If osteoporosis is not treated, an even more dangerous problem is that she may have a fall and break her hip joint, which will require urgent surgery and all the risks that come with surgery at an old age.

Case 9: Mild backache for six months, has pain in both legs when walking, now unable to walk more than 100 metres

A 65-year-old man, who had mild backache for a few months, has been suffering from worsening pain for a few days. He cannot walk more than 100 metres because he gets pain in both legs, with feelings of pins and needles. The leg is less painful when he sits down. He cannot stand more than five minutes before he has to sit down.

On examination, he will not have much tenderness in the back or buttocks. He may have evidence of wear and tear osteoarthritis in other joints.

This patient has classical symptoms of the narrowing of the spinal canal (spinal stenosis). An X-ray will show that degenerative changes of the spine and osteoarthritis of the facet joints, causing the spinal canal to be narrowed. The spinal nerves are thus compressed into a narrow spinal canal. If he is not active (e.g. sitting or lying down), the nerves are able to manage in the tight space. But once he stands up for long periods or begins to walk, the limited spinal space is insufficient for the smooth working of the nerves. He thus develops pain in the legs, with the feeling of pins and needles (paresthesia). The typical history is that the nerve symptoms get better when he sits or lies down.

The treatment is to try the simple methods first as in Case #6.

He may benefit from medication to strengthen his nerves, as well as physiotherapy like deep heat to the lower spine and buttock area. If the treatments are unsuccessful, he may then need inactivation of the trigger points in his muscles. Trigger point injections and prolotherapy can also be helpful.

If he is severely disabled, and cannot walk or stand for long periods, or if there is pain even when he is sitting or lying down, he should have a CT or MRI scan done to see how narrow the spinal canal has become. He may require surgery (laminectomy) to open up the space in his spinal canal to allow more freedom for the nerves. When done for the proper indications, surgery will give very good relief for patients with spinal stenosis.

Case 10: Mild back pain for the last six months, suddenly very painful

A 65-year-old man, who had mild backache for a few months, has been suffering from worsening pain for a few days. He can still walk around but the pain at night affects his sleep. He has been smoking two packs of cigarettes a day for nearly 40 years. He has never injured his spine or had backache before.

On examining him, he has tenderness (pain on direct pressure) on one central spot in the low back. He looks thin and weak. He says he is losing weight. He has had cough for 20 years.

In older people with this type of backache, we must suspect possible cancer. Usually, the cancer will come from another area and in this patient, we must think of lung cancer in view of his history of smoking. Thus, in older patients, X-rays are usually done to make sure there is no bone problem.

In this man, one of the lumbar vertebra shows a collapse consistent with cancer. He is a smoker, so a chest X-ray is also done, and it shows cancer in the lung. This patient needs to see a cancer specialist for treatment.

If a patient has had cancer before (e.g. cancer from the lung, breast, thyroid, kidney, prostate or intestines), and is now having backache, an X-ray must be done. It is also justifiable to do an MRI scan.

Section V

Pictorial Charts

Back Exercise Charts

14

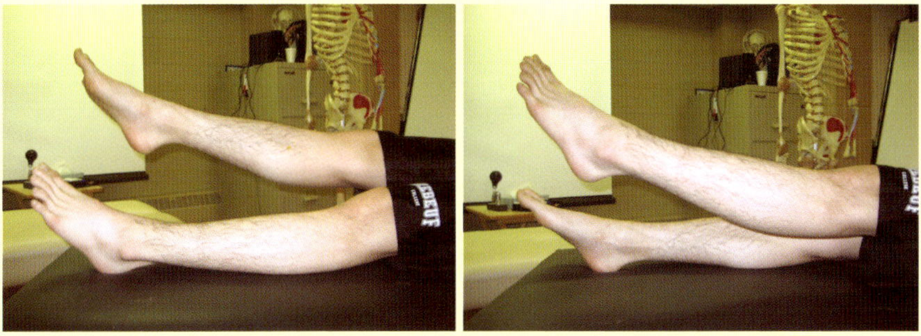

Exercise 14.1: Abdominal Strengthening

Lie flat on a moderately firm surface, lift the right leg (knee straight) about 6 inches off the bed, hold for about 5 seconds, and put it down. Repeat with the left leg. Repeat this simple exercise 10 times. Do this exercise daily.

Simple exercises like these are meant to tone the abdominal and some related muscles. It will not cause the muscle to become bulky. It is surprising how this and the other simple exercises help in the long term to reduce the incidence of recurrent back pain. The biggest problem is that patients tend to forget doing exercises once the back pain has subsided.

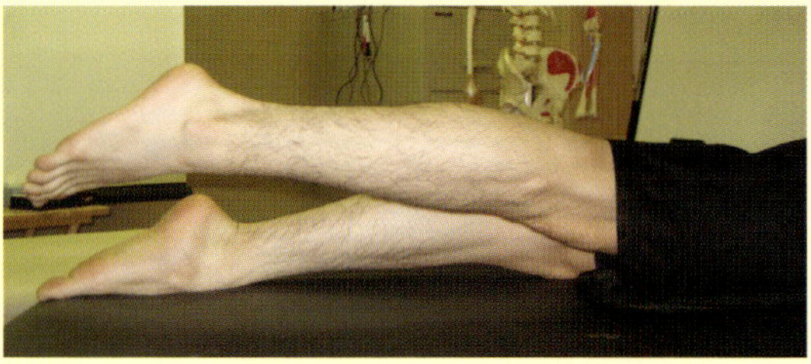

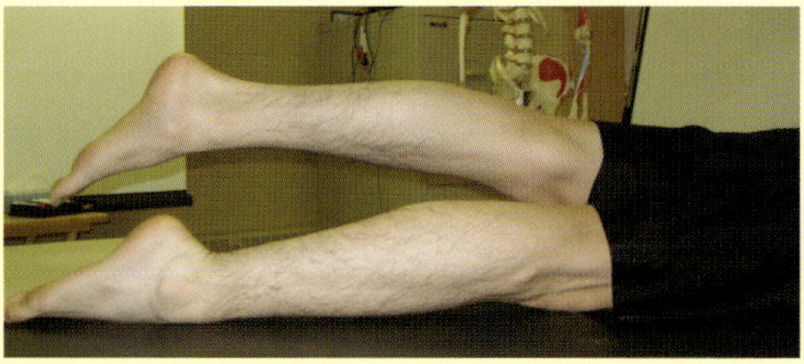

Exercise 14.2: General Back Strengthening

Lie on your stomach, on a moderately firm surface, lift the right leg (knee straight) about 6 inches above the bed, hold for 5 seconds and put it down. Repeat with the left leg. Repeat this exercise 10 times. Do this daily after Exercise 14.1.

Again, this simple exercise is to maintain muscle tone and strength. If done regularly with the other exercises, these exercises can protect the back from muscle tensions and inflammations.

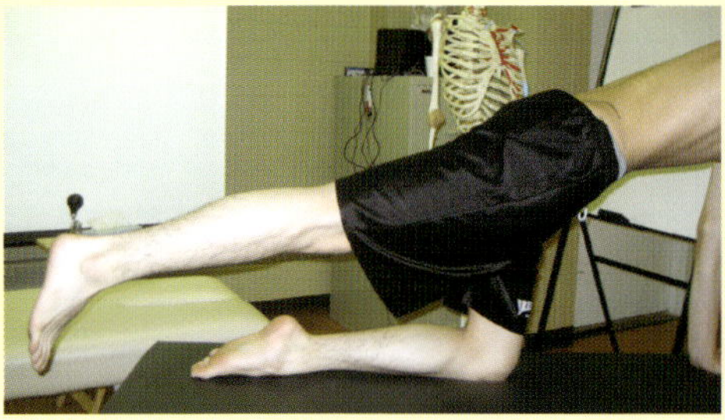

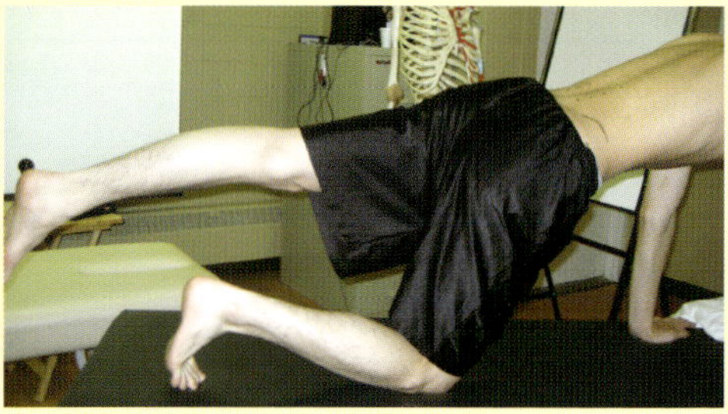

Exercise 14.3: Back Strengthening (Multifidus Muscle)

Get on all fours, lift the right leg up (with knee straight) as shown, bring the leg down after 2 to 5 seconds. Repeat with the left leg. Repeat the sequence 10 times with each leg.

The multifidus is a deep muscle that supports the spine. It is a group of muscles, and is the one targeted in trigger point injections and prolotherapy.

Weakness of the multifidus can give rise to chronic (mild to moderate) back pain. Do these exercises regularly and it will help prevent the recurrence of back pain.

Back Exercises

Erector Spinae

Back Facing Up

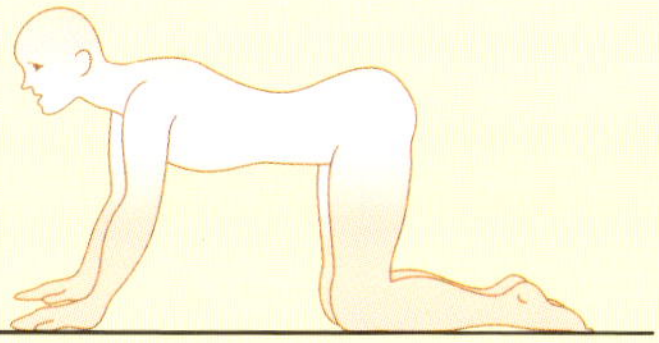

(a)

(b)

Back Lying Down

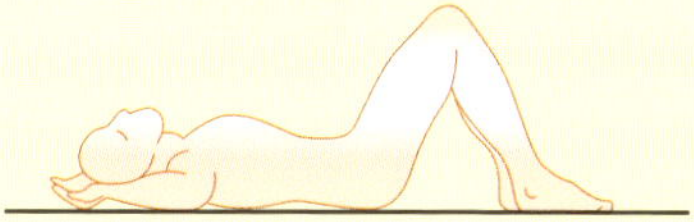

(a)

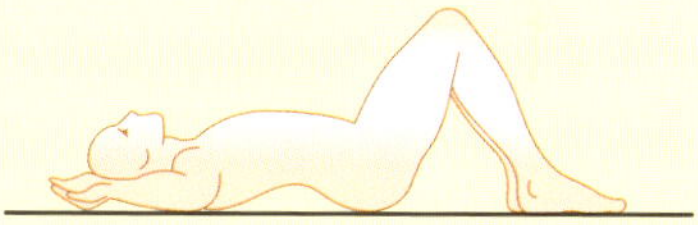

(b)

Exercise 14.4: Back Strengthening

Start at position (a). Raise the body to position (b) and hold for 2 to 5 seconds. Come back to original position. Repeat the sequence 10 times.

This exercise strengthens the superficial to multifidus muscle group. It is a good exercise to further support the spine and keep a good muscle tone. By doing these exercises regularly, there will be a decrease in the areas of inflammation and spasm. Back pain will be reduced and recurrences minimised.

These back exercises may seem simple and many patients tend to forget to do them once they are pain free. But by investing only 10 minutes a day to these exercises, the rewards will be great.

15

Back Stretching Charts

Back Extension Stretch

Back Flexion Stretch

Photo 15.1: Back Stretches

Place hands on the hips, bend backwards as far as you comfortably can. Then, bend forward as shown. Repeat the sequence 10 times.

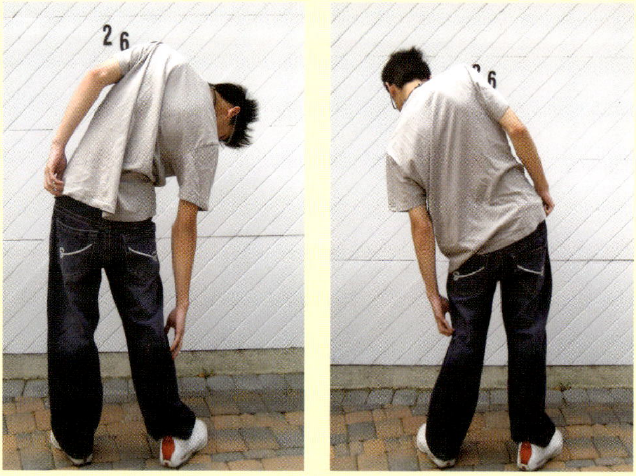

Photo 15.2: Side Bending Stretch

This is a lateral stretch exercise. Stand with your right arm hanging by the side, bend to the right as far as you can. Then, bend to the left. Repeat the exercise 10 times.

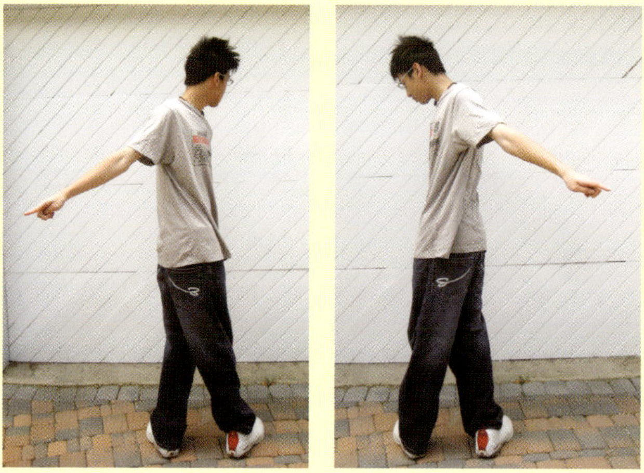

Photo 15.3: Rotation Stretch

This exercises maintains rotatory flexibility of the spine.

Start with your arms hanging by the side, lift your right arm and rotate the body as far as you comfortably can. Return to the starting position, rotate to the left side as shown. Repeat the sequence 10 times daily.

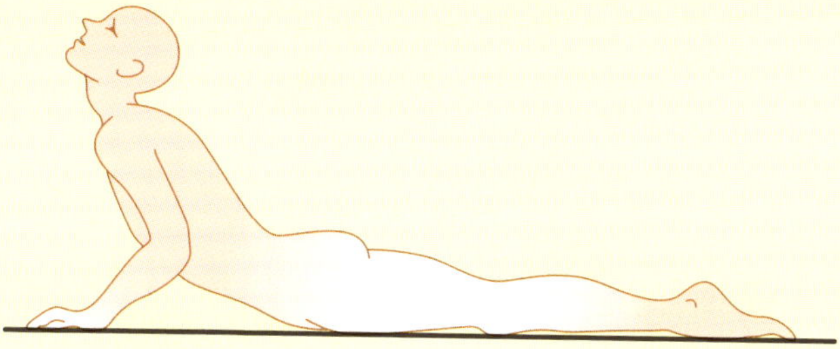

Diagram 15.4: Abdominal Stretch
Lie on the stomach, lift your body up on the hands as shown. Use arm power to stretch the abdominal muscles. Come back to prone position. Repeat 10 times daily.

Trigger Point Injection Charts

16

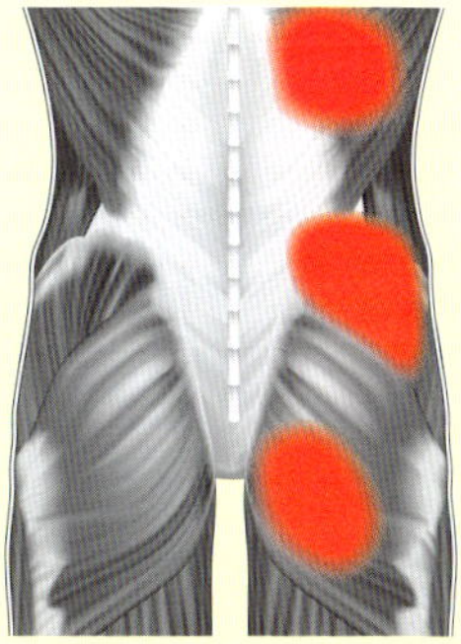

Erector Spinae Muscles

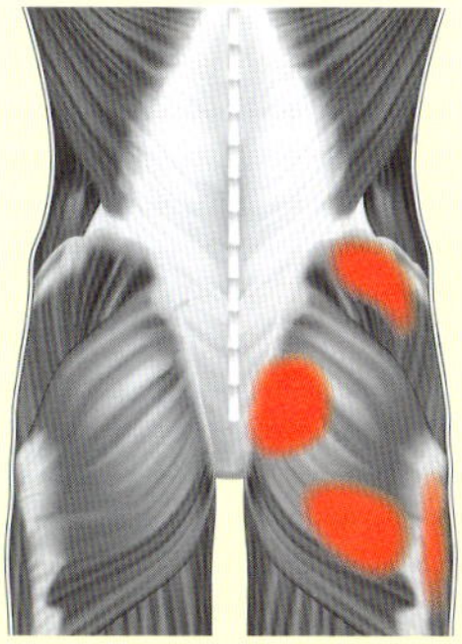

Quadratus Lumborum Muscles

Diagram 16.1: Lumbago — Non-specific Low Back Pain

Pain is felt in the marked areas when these back muscles are weak, inflamed or have painful nodules (spasm).

Deep massage or manipulation, and/or physiotherapy can help reduce the pain. In cases where recovery is slow or where the pain is severe, the trigger points in those areas (most tender area) are injected. Many chronic pain sufferers find great improvement with injection and physiotherapy.

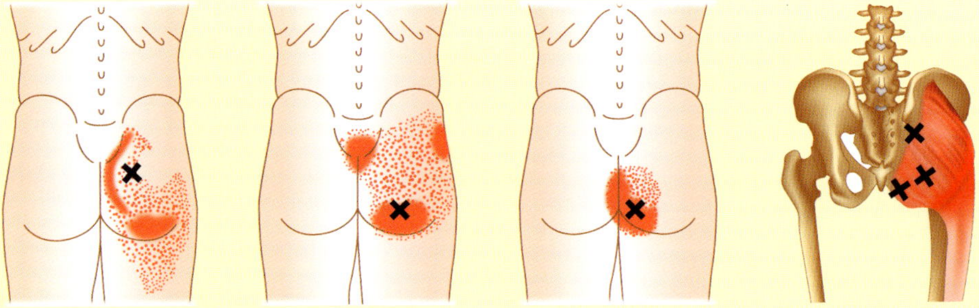

Diagram 16.2: One-sided Low Back Pain Caused by Painful Gluteus Maximus Trigger Points

The three pictures on the left show the areas where many patients may complain of back or buttock pain. This pain is often worse when sitting for long periods. The pain can be aggravated when bending forward to lift a heavy load, or even to pick up a light object.

The diagram on the right shows the Gluteus Maximus muscle. It is one of the largest muscles in the body and is an important extensor of the hip joint. Weakness of the muscles and the stress of daily walking or standing can result in inflammation of the gluteus muscle. This results in tender nodules that cause the chronic pain. The way to diagnose this condition is to (a) stretch the muscle by flexing the hip and (b) apply deep pressure at the points marked (X). Acute pain on deep pressure is highly suggestive of gluteus maximus strain and spasm.

Injection of the tender trigger point nodules results in rapid and significant improvement of symptoms. Many patients who have become depressed due to chronic back pain have recovered and have had their lives transformed. The patients must then continue gluteal stretching and strengthening exercises to prevent the return of the pain. Physiotherapy or massage therapy is also helpful to protect against recurrence.

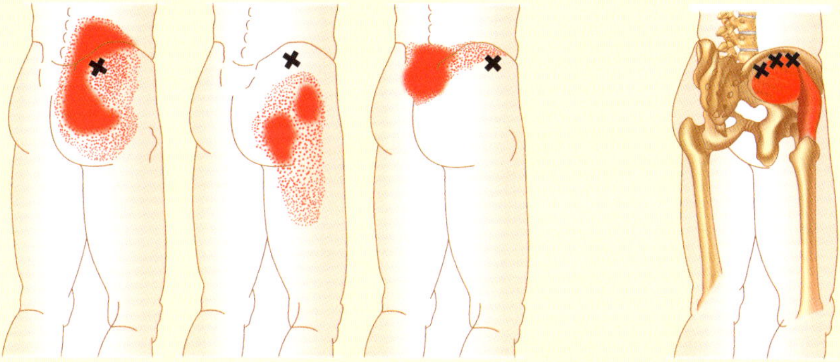

Diagram 16.3: Low Back Pain Caused by Painful Gluteus Medius Trigger Points

The gluteus medius muscle lies under the gluteus maximus. It is a strong abductor of the hip joint (lifting the leg sideways away from the midline). A weak gluteus medius is a cause of pain during walking. Gluteus medius inflammation, with tender nodules, gives rise to pain in the areas marked (the three pictures on the left above).

The pain from gluteus medius problems can mimic non-specific low back pain. Many cases wrongly diagnosed as lumbar strain or intervetebral disc injury are actually gluteus muscle problems. Once a prolapsed disc is ruled out, a careful examination of the muscles will be positive for tender areas (marked X in the picture on the right).

Gluteus medius strain with painful nodules is the most common cause of chronic back pain seen in my clinic for the past two decades. Most of these patients have been treated for months or years by both allopathic and alternative medicine, but the pain does not go away, or it resolves for a short while, then keeps coming back. Trigger point injection usually gives good results and with proper stretching, physiotherapy and muscle exercises, most patients do not get problems again.

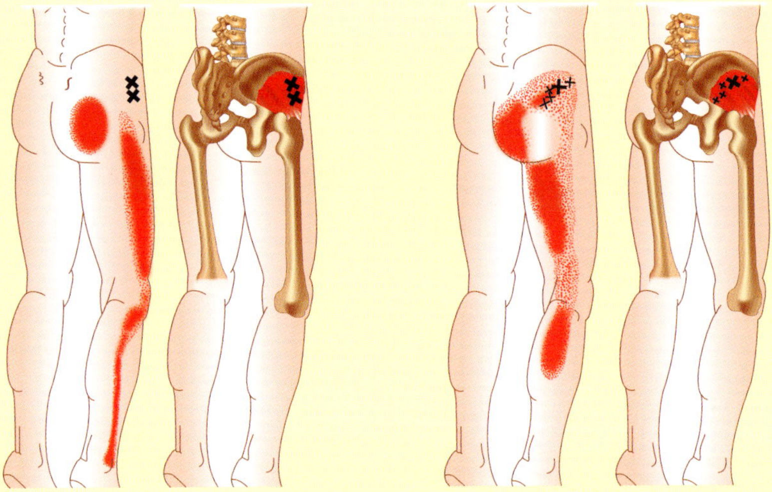

Diagram 16.4: Sciatica Type Symptoms Caused by Painful Gluteus Minimus Trigger Points

The pictures on the left show the area where the patient complains of pain (areas marked in red).

The pain mimics sciatica — the condition where the nerve is compressed in the spine, most often due to a prolapsed intervertebral disc. Many patients have been treated for prolapsed disc, and it is no surprise that they do not recover. Many patients have tried Western and alternative medicine without relief.

Since the problem arises in the gluteus muscles (particularly the gluteus minimus), the treatment must target this area. I always check any patient complaining of sciatic type pain for tenderness in the trigger point areas marked (X), and almost all my patients respond to injections of these trigger points.

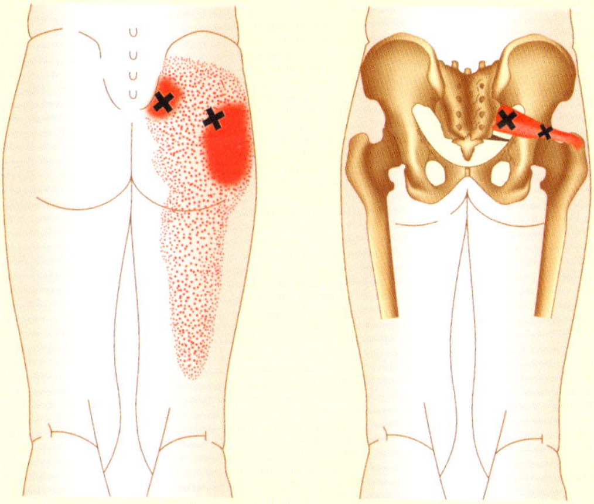

Diagram 16.5: Back Pain Radiating to Upper Thigh (Piriformis Syndrome)

The picture on the right shows a short muscle called the piriformis. The sciatic nerve runs over this muscle. In rare cases, the sciatic nerve runs through the nerve. Any tightness or inflammation of the piriformis muscle can mimic the radiating pain of a nerve compression. The (X) marks the tenderness in the piriformis muscle.

I usually ask the patient to turn to the side and flex (bend) the hip to 90 degrees. This stretches the piriformis muscle and allows me to look for tenderness and painful nodules in the muscles. A correct diagnosis greatly helps to solve the chronic pain suffered by many.

Injections of the sites marked (X) have given rapid relief to patients who have been treated as a slipped disc and/or tried many Western and alternative medicine without success.

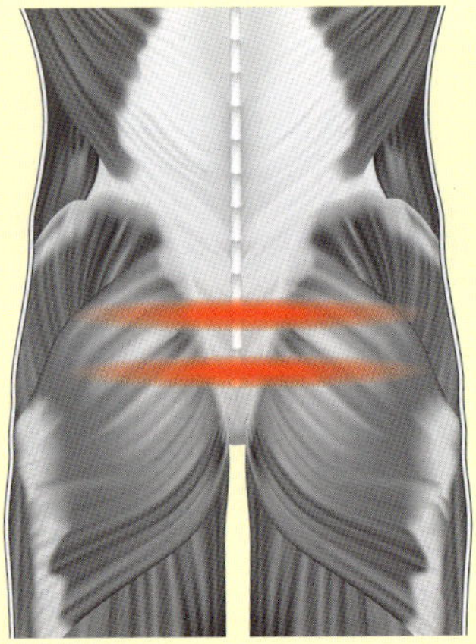

Diagram 16.6: Non-specific Back Pain — Weak Abdominals
Weak or scarred abdominal muscles can surprisingly give rise to a backache as marked. The pain is non-specific and vague, and may even cause family and friends to doubt whether there is really a back problem.

Exercises to strengthen the abdominal muscles and to improve flexibility will usually solve this problem. Sometimes, the posterior part of the abdominal muscles may require an injection and/or physiotherapy. Once recovered, patients should ideally continue with exercises and stretching.

Section VI

Recommended Reading

Recommended Reading

Any treatment can be initiated based on two possible presuppositions:

1. *Anecdotal Evidence* — when a treatment is recommended based on one person's testimony or what has been passed down over the years or claimed to be a new discovery.

2. *Evidence-based Medicine* — is backed by research that is conducted on a particular treatment by studying two groups of patients — one group given the treatment and the other not given the treatment. If there is a statistically significant improvement in the treatment group, then that treatment is deemed useful for the back pain.

Modern textbooks now include research studies from multiple sources. It is unwise to believe the research done only by the company that is selling a product or treatment. **Always look at whether there is evidence-based conclusions from more than one source.** The following books or articles may be useful for detailed study:

General Information

- David A Wong and Ensor Transfeldt, *MacNab's Backache* (Philadelphia: Lippincott Williams Wilkins, 2006).

A useful textbook on backache. It expands on all the aspects of backache for a medical professional or health practitioner. Many other good textbooks are available.

Physical Therapy, Exercise and Alternative Modalities

- Chad Cook, *Orthopedic Manual Therapy: An Evidence-Based Approach* (Upper Saddle River, NJ: Prentice Hall, 2006).
- Jeffrey D Placzek and David A Boyce, *Orthopaedic Physical Therapy Secrets,* 2nd edition (St. Louis, MO: Hanley and Belfus, 2006).
- Carol Kisner and Lynn Allen Colby, *Therapeutic Exercise: Foundations and Techniques*, 5th edition (Philadelphia, PA: FA Davis, 2007).
- Edzard Ernst, Max H Pittler and Barbara Wider, *The Desktop Guide to Complementary and Alternative Medicine: An Evidence-Based Approach*, 2nd edition (Philadelphia, PA: Mosby, 2006).

These are comprehensive reviews with evidence-based information, useful for professionals in that particular field. The books give detailed information on the studies that support the use of the different modalities, and on why some modalities are used in certain circumstances.

Orthopaedic Injection Techniques

- Stephanie Saunders and Steve Longworth, *Injection Techniques in Orthopaedics and Sports Medicine with CD-ROM: A Practical Manual for Doctors and Physiotherapists*, 3rd edition (Edinburgh: Churchill Livingstone, 2006).

This book explains why and where injections are done, what solutions are used, types of steroids and local anaesthetics and how they are injected. This is useful since there are many unfounded fears about orthopaedic injection techniques. In the United Kingdom, tens of thousands of such injections are given every year. Many elderly chronic back pain patients are able to be active due to this treatment.

Trigger Point Inactivation

- DJ Simons, Janet G Travell and LS Simons, *Myofascial Pain and Dysfunction: The Trigger Point Manual Vol. 1 and 2* (Philadelphia: Lippincort Williams & Wilkins, 1999).

This comprehensive two-volume work explains the rationale and scientific basis for trigger point injection and inactivation. It explains the markedly increased pressure within the trigger zones and how the pain is caused, and demonstrates where injections are given for chronic low back pain.

Prolotherapy Techniques

- Thomas H Ravin, Mark S Cantieri and George J Pasquarello, *Principles of Prolotherapy* (Denver, CO: American Academy of Manual Medicines, 2008).
- Ross A Hauser and Marion A Hauser, *Prolo Your Back Pain Away: Curing Chronic Back Pain with Prolotherapy* (Beulah Land Press, 2000).

The first book is a comprehensive manual for doctors and a systematic review of the principles and techniques of prolotherapy, while the second is a more readable book for patients and medical professionals. It includes information on the solutions used for injections, the common ligaments and tissues that are injected, and the estimated recovery time.

Spinal Decompression

- Dwain M Daniel, "Non-surgical Spinal Decompression Therapy: Does the Scientific Literature Support Efficacy Claims Made in the Advertising Media?" Available at http://www.pubmedcentral.nih.gov/articlerender.fcgi?artid=1887522) *Journal Chiropractice and Osteopathy*. 2007, 15: 7; Internet; accessed 2 Aug 2009.

A useful study on the advertised benefits of spinal decompression. This independent study does not back spinal decompression as an alternative to simple treatments. It considers spinal decompression to be just another incarnation of traction therapy.

Footwear and Back Pain

- Lee C-M, Jeong E-H and Freivalds A, "Biomechanical Effects of Wearing High-heeled Shoes," *International Journal of Industrial Ergonomics* 2001, 28: 321-326.

An ergonomic study of the stresses of wearing high heels in women. The increased pressure on the spine and forefoot is significant and women are advised to wear such heels for short periods only.

Stress and Psychological Effects on Low Back Pain

- Bruce S McEwen, "Physiology and Neurobiology of Stress and Adaptation: Central Role of the Brain," *Physiology Revue* 2007, 87: 873-904.
- George R Hansen and Jon Streltzer, "The Psychology of Pain," *Emergency Medicine Clinics of North America*, 2005 May, 23(2).
- Marwan N Baliki, Dante R Chialvo, Paul Y Geha, Robert M Levy, R Norman Harden, Todd B Parrish and A Vania Apkarian, "Chronic Pain and the Emotional Brain: Specific Brain Activity Associated with Spontaneous Fluctuations of Intensity of Chronic Back Pain," *The Journal of Neuroscience*, 2006 Nov 22, 26(47):12165-12173.

There is ample evidence-based studies to show that there are real physical problems consequent to psychological factors caused by stress, anxiety and depression. Studies on brain imaging and on how stress (called the allostatic load by professionals) and the brain's maldaptive reaction to the situation can cause back pain are detailed.

Index

F

H

I

L

M

N

O

P

S

T

U

V

X